Python 3 Without Prior Knowledge

Learn how to program a neural network within 7 days

Imprint:

PBD  Verlag

Author: Benjamin Spahic
Konradin-Kreutzer-Str. 12
76684 Östringen
Gemany
Editor/ Proofreading: Mentorium GmbH
Cover: Kim Nusko
ISBN Paperback: 9798481269184

Email: Benjamin-Spahic@web.de

Python Without Prior Knowledge
First publication 15.12.2020
Distribution through kindledirectpublishing
Amazon Media EU S.à r.l., 5 Rue Plaetis, L-2338, Luxembourg

Content

1. Preface and introduction

In the last 50 years, humanity has experienced a revolution rarely seen in previous history.

No other development has had such a gigantic impact on the productivity and well-being of the entire world population.

We are talking about digitalisation, which is still ongoing. Thanks to this technological progress, we can lead the life we do. We work in front of screens or communicate with the help of our smartphones. At the same time, countless factories full of robots and conveyor belts produce goods and commodities.

All this is only possible through years of research and development and the perfect interaction of hardware and software. The hardware includes the microprocessors, computers and electrical components, which are finally given life by the adapted software, the installation of the programme or the programme code. The two go hand in hand and without one the other is worthless. Hardware is becoming more and more affordable. At the same time, the computing power of processors is multiplying.

This also increases the demand for programmers for the machines and creates numerous new jobs in this sector, which, however, cannot always be filled. Large companies like Bosch, Siemens or SAP have been permanently looking for well-trained, highly qualified computer scientists for years. The well-known car manufacturers also have an acute shortage of programmers for their control units, safety systems, etc.

The reason for this is a serious enthusiasm problem in our society. Almost everyone uses technology and benefits from progress, but few have the will to understand electrical engineering and programming and become part of the inventor community.

However, since you have bought this book, you seem to be interested in exactly this subject area. And that leads us to the core topic of this book - programming in Python.

Python is currently one of the simplest programming languages and is therefore becoming increasingly popular, both in the private sector and in industry. Programming in Python is beginner-friendly, application-based, quick to learn and there is a large community whose members are available for support if you have questions about specific topics. If you stumble at any point, you can find help in the official Python forum, countless blog posts or YouTube videos.

Maybe you're a student looking into programming a robot, an electrical engineer who wants to learn more about software, or a young-at-heart retiree interested in programming in general.

In any case, you will not regret dealing with the matter.

Certainly, there are many websites and books that introduce you to the topic of Python programming. However, some of these books are over 500 pages long and completely unsuitable for newcomers.

If one is already somewhat familiar with the subject and needs pointers for a specific project, such textbooks can be helpful, but for a large proportion of prospective students they are neither necessary nor effective.

And it is precisely this problem that gave rise to this book.

It is a beginner's guide for those who want to learn the basics of Python programming without much prior knowledge in order to start their first project as soon as possible.

To do this, the following questions are clarified first: Which programmes and libraries do I need? How do I programme my own functions? What needs to be considered? All this is worked out step by step and rounded off with a real example project.

The name Python is not derived from the snake species, but from a British cult TV show called Monty Python's Flying Circus from the early 1970s.

Dutch inventor Guido van Rossum was a big fan of the show. This is also reflected in many of his documentaries and learning materials on the programming language, which feature quotes from the TV show.

Prerequisites and level of knowledge:

This book is suitable for anyone with a basic enthusiasm for IT and programming. The basic knowledge of programming such as syntax, the flow of a programme etc. is important and is therefore listed in the first chapters.

Programming experience from other languages or other previous knowledge is not assumed. This manual is also explicitly aimed at beginners and programming novices.

For a better structure, the following icons can be found again and again at certain points in the book:

Light bulb: Here the key points of a chapter are summarised. These statements are good for reference or when reviewing a topic.

 Attention: Common mistakes are mentioned at this point. It explains which obstacles can occur where and why and which assumptions are often erroneous

 The calculator is used for example calculations or comprehension questions for comprehension and internalisation.

Notation in this book:

Terms in bold: Terms that are to be newly introduced or particularly emphasised.

Italicised terms: Variable names, functions and other terms that are to be set off from the continuous text.

Now I hope you enjoy reading and diving into Python programming.

2. Preparation - Install interpreter and text editor

Python 3 is the successor to Python 2, which was released in 2000 and is still widely used. However, Python 3, which is 8 years younger, is gaining more and more market share and will replace the previous version in the long term.

Since 2020, Python 2 has no longer been developed or supported, which is why it is clearly the better choice for newcomers to start directly with Python 3. This version has the advantage that it codes completely in Unicode. This means that special characters and umlauts are displayed correctly. We will see that umlauts such as Ö, Ä, Ü appear again and again later in the examples without having to rewrite them. All in all, Python 3 is the future. Large companies like Instagram and Facebook are currently switching from Python 2 to Python 3.

In order to start programming, we first need to install some software on our computer. First, we have to download the programmes that are needed for Python programming. These include a text editor and an interpreter. What exactly an interpreter is will be explained in more detail later. First, we need a suitable text editor.

2.1. The text editor

A programme code is nothing more than the stringing together of several words, designations and variables in a certain form and with a defined structure.

A programme (source code) can initially be described simply as a multiline text.

 A programme code can be opened and edited in an ordinary text editor. You do not need a special programme for this.

The logical consequences of the instructions subsequently become understandable through the interpretation.

So, to write a programme in Python we can use any text editor.

However, it is advisable to use a text editor, which is intended for programming. Microsoft Word is also a word processing programme, but it clearly focuses on the visual appearance of a text. This is helpful for a term paper or a manuscript, but rather annoying for programming. The reason for this is that all the details such as layout and page height are also saved in the files and they therefore contain an unnecessarily large amount of information for programming.

The standard Windows editor (Notepad) is already much more oriented towards programming but does not support many functions that are important for programming. Linux users already have an extensive editor on board with gEdit. For Windows users, who will be most of us, we recommend the tool NotepadPlusPlus (Notepad++). The programme is suitable for various programming languages. Signal words are highlighted in colour and some error messages are recognised automatically. The disadvantage is that you cannot execute the programme directly. Especially for beginners, a quick ready-to-go solution is advisable.

In the context of this book, we use the editor **Anaconda.** This is an open source project for the programming languages Python and R. Anaconda is also used at schools and universities because it is particularly beginner-friendly.

 Anaconda is a complete package consisting of the **Spyder** development environment, the **IPhython** interpreter and other components. This also saves the additional installation of an interpreter. But what is an interpreter anyway?

An interpreter, usually together with a compiler, takes over the "translation" and interpretation of the programme code. The way it works is complex and is therefore presented in a simplified way. Basically, a programming language needs a suitable interpreter adapted to it.

In our case, we therefore use IPython, which is installed directly with Anaconda.

IPython will later convert our programme code in the background into commands that the computer can then execute.

Before we get to the first programme, we must first download the package that contains a graphical user interface and the interpreter. The tool is made available by various third-party providers, but it is also advisable here to download Anaconda from the official website.

2.2. Installation of Anaconda

The current version of Anaconda can be downloaded from https://www.ana-conda.com/products/individual.

Figure 1 Anaconda Installers

For this, we can select the version suitable for our operating system. Since Windows systems are the most common, the installation is shown using Windows. The procedure is analogous for the other platforms.

Figure 2 Anaconda Setup

After the successful installation of Anaconda, the development interface Spyder can be opened. To do this, we search for the Spyder programme in the Windows search bar. The following window opens.

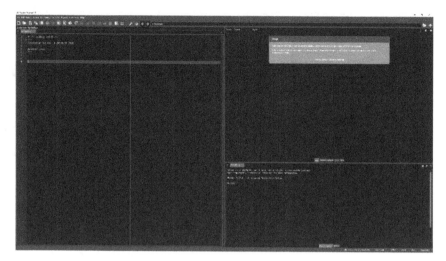

Figure 3 Spyder user interface

As already mentioned, this is the user interface in which we can write our programme. At the same time, Spyder offers many other advantages as a scientifically oriented environment.

 The Spyder development interface offers considerably more possibilities than are necessary for a beginner. However, it is advisable to get used to a scientifically oriented development environment right away in order to benefit from the advantages later.

However, Spyder is also especially suitable for beginners. **Keywords** are automatically recognised and displayed in colour. This makes different programming elements such as variables, comments, functions or classes stand out from each other. What exactly is meant by these terms will be explained in the next chapters.

```
    Klassen.py*
1   '''Übung Klassen und Vererbung'''
2   class Mensch:
3       def _init_(self,name,alter,größe,):
4           self.Name=name    #Speichern der übergebenen Variablen
5           self.Alter=alter
6           self.größe=größe
7
```

Figure 4 coloured keyword recognition in Spyder

Normal variables and commands have a white background. Comments are automatically greyed out and signal words are coloured.

Once Anaconda or Spyder is open, we could theoretically start programming directly.

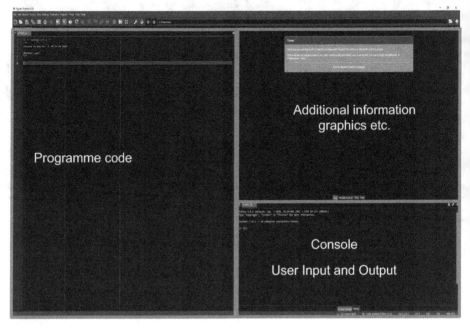

Figure 5 The different elements of Spyder

The programme code is written in the left-hand window, the **console,** the interface between the user and the computer, can be found in the lower right-hand window. Error messages, for example, are output in the console.

In the upper right window, further information such as illustrations or variables are displayed. This is extremely helpful, especially for troubleshooting later and is another advantage of Spyder.

To execute the programme code written here, we click on the large green arrow in the upper task bar. This starts the programme once. Alternatively, a programme can be executed by pressing CTRL+ENTER.

The other icons next to the start button have other functions, such as automatically restarting the programme after the first run. These buttons are of no interest to us at first.

Figure 6 Running a programme

 Before starting the programme, you should save it in a folder of your choice and give it a meaningful name. The extension of a Python file is always .py.

Before moving on to the actual code creation, the structure of a Python programme is explained.

3. Programming - the most important building blocks

The basics of programming are explained below.

More specifically, the building blocks such as using comments, brackets or indentation are described using Python. The principles can also be transferred to other programming languages such as Java, C, C# and others. However, Python has the decisive advantage of focusing on clarity and simplicity. For example, unlike in other programming languages, there are rarely brackets or semicolons.

3.1. Comments

Comments serve the clarity and structure of a programme. If we write a programme and then do not use it for years, it will take us a very long time later to understand the functions again.

Therefore, comments are enormously important for a quick understanding of the function of a programme.

Comments serve as memory aids, structural elements and to explain the code.

-ʘ́- A comment is not translated by the compiler/interpreter. It only serves the human to better understand the programme.

Comments are headed with a **hash sign.**

```
# this is a comment
```

Comments are directly recognised as such by the text editor or the development environment. They are **greyed out in** Spyder.

There is no hard and fast rule as to when we should put a comment. When it comes to decision support, the saying *"better one comment too many than too few"* applies. Other programmers who want to understand our code, and we ourselves, will be grateful for every comment later.

3.2. Docstrings

For better clarity, it is advisable to provide a description of the programme in addition to the comments. These descriptions are called docstrings and make it easier for the programmer to understand the background and functioning of the programme. **Docstrings** can also be read out with special functions without having to access the source code.

Especially when several people are working on a project or several people need to understand the same code, comments and docstrings are essential.

An example could look like this:

''' Programme code: Python example program

Automation of a sorting station

Author: Max Mustermann

Created: 12.12.2021

Project status: 01.01.2022

'''

As seen in the example above, the comment section of the doc string is opened and closed with three single ''' or three double quotes """. The function is exactly the same.

""" Everything inside the inverted commas is interpreted as a heading/description.
"""

In the Spyder user environment, docstrings (green) and comments (grey) are automatically recognised and highlighted in colour.

 When copying and pasting code, for example from internet pages or other programmes, it can happen that the inverted commas are not taken over correctly. The programmer must then delete them and enter them again.

Now we know how important it is to document a programme sufficiently and how to set the comments and docstrings. The next step is the concrete programming of means instructions.

3.3. Instructions

Instructions form the core of a programme. "Instruction" is an umbrella term for, for example, arithmetic operations or input or output commands at the console. Defining variables, calling functions or breaking a loop is also an instruction. With instructions, it is advisable to append a comment again.

 Statements can be written one below the other. Through the new line, the interpreter recognises that it is a new instruction.

```
Instruction1 #Comment on Instruction1

Instruction2 #Comment on instruction2

Instruction3 #Comment on Instruction3
```

Alternatively, we can write several instructions in the same line. In this case, they are separated by a semicolon. This makes sense if two instructions logically belong together closely or if we often call the same instruction.

```
Instruction1 ; Instruction2 #Comment on Instruction1 and 2
```

The first easy-to-understand instruction introduced is the call to the *print()* function.

3.4. Console output with print()

The *print()* function is one of the simplest and most used functions. With its help, one can output values at the console. This gives us a way to "communicate" with the user of the programme.

With the *print()* command, words and numbers can be output to the console, as well as the contents of variables, lists or whole data sets, which are discussed in the following chapter.

In the first example, we pass a text to the function that is to be displayed to the user. We put this text between the round brackets in the *print()* function.

The text to be output is placed inside the brackets in single or double quotes.

```
print("Hello World") #puts Hello World in the console
```

Remember, in order for the programme to start, it must be executed via the button with the green arrow.

If you want to output the double inverted commas as well, you can put single inverted commas in front of them.

```
print('"Hello World"') #puts out "Hello World
```

As already mentioned, we can not only output pure text, but also numbers or whole calculations.
Unlike text, the inverted commas are omitted when outputting a calculation. Thus, the result of the mathematical operation is output and not the text characters of the calculation. An example illustrates this:

```
print("3+4") #The output is 3+4
```

```
print(3+4) #7 is output
```

```
In [1]: runfile('C:/Python_examples/Chapter 3 - Basics/001 print.py', wdir='C:/Pyth
3+4
7
```

Figure 7 print output in the console

It is practical that after a *print()* command a break is automatically inserted in the console.

We have various options for displaying the output.

For an orderly appearance, additional paragraphs and blank lines can be inserted when outputting the data via an empty *print() command*.

print() #blank line

A line break can be realised with the character string \n , an indentation (tabulator) with the character string \t .

print('Paragraph follows\n') #paragraph

print('Blank line follows')

print() #blank line

print("\t This text is indented")

```
In [2]: runfile('C:/Python_examples/Chapter 3 - Basics/001 print.py', wdir='C:/
Python_examples/Chapter 3 - Basics')
Paragraph follows

Blank line follows

    this text is indented
```

Figure 8 Example print output of a paragraph, spaces and an indentation

Alternatively, a *print()* command can also be output over several lines.

This requires three inverted commas at the beginning and end of the text, just like a docstring.

Afterwards, the line breaks are also output in the console.

print('''this text

will

output

in 4 lines'')

```
In [3]: runfile('C:/Python_examples/Chapter 3 - Basics/001 print.py', wdir='C:/
Python_examples/Chapter 3 - Basics')
this text
will
output
in 4 lines
```

Figure 9 print output over several lines

After learning how to output simple text or numbers using the *print()* function, we next look at storing data in variables.

3.5. Variables

Variables are indispensable for almost every Python programme. They are numbers, characters or whole texts that can be changed during the runtime of a programme. They are used to store values. By naming the variables, we can retrieve the value during the course of the programme, for example to use it in a calculation.

A variable consists of a name and a value. We can imagine the variable as a box on which the name of the variable is written. The content is the value of the variable. This understanding will be important later.

 To create a variable, we simply write the name of the desired variable and assign it a value directly with the equal sign (assignment operator).

Unlike other programming languages, we do not have to initialise variables in Python at the beginning of a programme. On the contrary, a variable must be assigned a value directly the first time it is mentioned.

The name of the variable can be chosen at will during creation and can contain letters, digits and underscores. However, it must not begin with a digit.

variable_test_1 = 4

Here *variable_test_1 is* the name of the variable, and the digit 4 is its content/value.

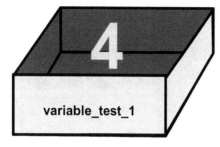

Figure 10Variable Box Model

There are some conventions in the creation of variable names which enable a programme to recognise within a few seconds which word represents a variable and which, for example, a class.

The most important conventions are:

- The name of a variable should reflect its function.

- Variables start with a lowercase letter.

- Variables consisting of more than one word are connected with an underscore

- Long words should be abbreviated whenever possible.

The naming of the variables should be meaningful and short. If there are several similar variables, it is advisable to distinguish them by name or by means of indices. For example, a variable in which a temperature value is stored could be called *temp1*.

temp1 = 20

temp2 = 30

...

The variable *temp1* (for example, indoors) is assigned the value 20. The variable *temp2* (for example, outdoors) is assigned the value 30.

The variables must be given unique names; a name may not be assigned more than once. In Python, an additional distinction is made between upper and lower case. *Temp1*, *TEMP1* and *temp1* are interpreted as three different variables.

Variables can also contain words (strings).

name = 'Tom

If we want to store words or sentences in a variable, we always have to put in-verted commas. We can use single or double inverted commas. The function is the same.

```
name = 'Tom
```

```
name = "Tom
```

Unlike in German, both inverted commas must be at the top.

The value of a variable can also be output with the *print()* function.

```
print(temp1)
```

When outputting variables via the *print()* function, there are a few things to con-sider with regard to the syntax.

If you want to print the content of a variable, no inverted commas are written. I.e. without inverted commas, the *print()* command expects a variable that must be defined.

If, on the other hand, the text is to be output, inverted commas must be used. The following table illustrates this with a few examples. First, the variable *name is* assigned the value *Tom.*

```
name='Tom' # The variable "name" is assigned the content 'Tom'.
```

print('name')	outputs "name
print(name)	spends "Tom
print(Tom)	Error, the variable "Tom" is not defined

The last call returns an error because no inverted commas are set. The function requests a variable at this point. However, the variable *Tom* is not known. *Tom* is merely the content of the variable *name*. This is an important difference.

The *print()* function can also display a combination of text and variables. This does not require multiple commands to be listed.

For example, if we want to specify the temperature including the unit °C, we can pack both into a *print() command.* The syntax is:

```
print("TEXT",VARIABLE, "TEXT")
```

The ranges are separated by a comma.

For the example of temperature, it looks like this:

```
temp1=20
```

```
print('Temperature: ',temp1,'°C')
```

```
In [1]: runfile('C:/Python_examples/Chapter 3 - Basics/002 print-temp1.py', wdir='C:/Python_exam
Temperature:   20 °C
```

The text is simply added to the variable by placing it in inverted commas.

But what happens when we want to save or output a quote?

For this, the interpreter must be informed that the inverted commas are to be regarded as text. To do this, we write a backslash (\) in front of the inverted comma.

This can be called up with the key combination **AltGr+ß**. This procedure is also called masking.

The inverted comma is masked as follows:

```
variable = 'This inverted comma \' has been masked'.
```

```
print(variable)
```

```
In [4]: runfile('C:/Python_examples/Chapter 3 - Basics/001 print.py', wdir='C:/Python_example
This quotation mark ' has been masked.
```

Now we know how to store numbers or words in variables and output them via the console. We have already gained a lot with this. In the next chapter we will deal with data types of variables and their classification.

3.6.   Data types

In every programming language, there are different types of variables that differ in terms of their height (memory requirements) or content.

This is referred to as data types. Different data are classified according to their type and function. A number, for example, has a different type than a word. But why do we need this distinction at all?

For example, if a variable can only contain the values 0 or 1, a single memory cell (bit) is sufficient to map the information. As an example, a coin toss can be chosen whose result can only take 1 (number) or 0 (heads).

It therefore makes no sense to provide the variable with 2, 3 or 10 memory cells. Therefore, the variable is assigned a data type that only occupies one memory cell and can only accept two values.

Besides housekeeping with storage units, there are other reasons why it makes sense to store data in different types.

For example, numbers can be calculated with the help of operators. $3 + 3 = 6$ is known and logically familiar to everyone. There is therefore a separate type for the data type "integers".

> Whole numbers are stored as **integers,** *int* for short. *The* interpreter knows: You can calculate with integer variables.

But what about words, for example?

> The data type for words is called ***string***. It is not as easy to calculate with as with integer variables.

A simple example illustrates the problem.

"Hello" + "World" # What does that add up to?

One could interpret the expression as "Hello world", although there is no mathematical basis for this. It becomes even clearer with a comparison.

"Hello" < "World" # What does this add up to?

This illustrates that you cannot apply arithmetic or logical operators to *string variables*.

Understanding the differences is essential for later chapters.

In addition to the two data types *string* and *int, there* are others. The following table lists the most important variable types with their properties. In addition, there are countless other variable types that play little or no role for newcomers.

Name	Abbreviation	Representation	Special feature
boolean	Bool	0 and 1 (True or False)	
string	Str	"Hello"	Strings

integer	Int	-1, 5, 1929	Only whole numbers
float	Float	1.32 ; 6.00 ; 128.28	(Floating) decimal numbers
List	List	[1,18,'Hello']	Multiple elements

In other programming languages, you have to tell the compiler which data type a variable is assigned to.

Not so with Python. The advantage of Python lies above all in the simple assignment of data types. Python recognises by means of the variables themselves which data type is to be used. A data type is automatically assigned by the content or the way the content is written, without having to specify it separately.

x = 5   *Variable is saved as an integer*

x = 5.00   *Variable is saved as a floating point number (float).*

x = "5.00"   *# Variable is saved as a character string (string)*

 Data types are not rigid. This means that they can also be changed within the programme.

Python also adjusts the data type here if necessary. If an integer (int) is offset against a floating point number (float), the result is automatically assigned a floating point number (float).

i = 52 # The data type is automatically set to integer

i = 52 + 0.01 # The data type is changed to float.

i = "fifty-two" # The data type is now a string

Each data type has different **attributes** (properties). This will be of importance in the chapter on functions, because not every function accepts all data types.

 With Spyder you can display the variables and their contents as well as the data type. This is especially helpful when searching for errors. Under the item **Variable Explorer** in the upper right field, the variable name, the data type as well as the length and content of the variables are displayed.

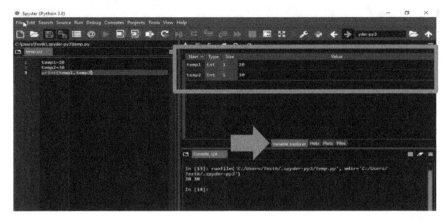

Figure 12Displaying data types in Spyder

In the example shown, the data type is integer (int).

It is advisable to consider a few things about the data types. What type results when we calculate 6 divided by 3? What type when we divide 7 by 3?

3.7. User input via input()

We have already learned how to output data to the console. Next, we will look at how we can request data from the user.

 The **input()** function serves exactly this purpose. It is helpful to involve the user of the programme during runtime.

You can also pass a request as an argument to the function.

```
input("Please enter a number between 0 and 10")
```

As soon as the programme executes the function, the prompt is issued in the console and it asks for user input. The user input is also done via the console. A number, a word or even sentences can be typed in. By pressing the Enter key, the data is read in.

The *input()* function saves the data input as a string. This is correct for words or sentences and can be adopted in this way.

 However, if you want to read in numbers in order to calculate with them afterwards, you have to use the function *eval()*.

 The function eval() saves the read-in data under the correct data type. Because we remember that we cannot calculate with *string variables.*

Now it gets a bit more complicated: We pass the complete *input() function* as an argument to the *eval()* function. We nest the functions inside each other.

If we want to store an entered value in a variable with the appropriate data type, the complete command is:

```
x= eval(input("Please enter a number between 0 and 10"))
```

This will output the prompt, then read in the number and convert it to the appropriate data type (integer) and store it in the variable *x*.

3.8. Round with round

When processing and reading in numbers, it often happens that a number is stored as a floating-point number. The *float* data type is accurate to several decimal places. This is very practical for calculations, but it is visually very unattractive for screen output. A simple example illustrates the problem.

```
y= 5/3
```

```
print(y)
```

```
In [7]: runfile('C:/Python_examples/Chapter 3 - Basics/003 round.py', wdir='C:/Py
1.6666666666666667
```

Figure 13Output of a float number

The *round()* function provides a remedy. The syntax is as follows

round(The number to round, number of decimal places)

```
y=5/3
```

```
print(round(y,2)) y is rounded to 2 decimal places.
```

```
In [8]: runfile('C:/Python_examples/Chapter 3 - Basics/003 round.py', wdir='C:/
1.67
```

Figure 14Output of a rounded float number

There are many more functions, which we will also become more familiar with and even write them ourselves. Before that, however, we will take a closer look at how to effectively store and process data.

3.9. Data type conversion

We have already learned about different data types and how Python processes them. Most of the time, the correct data type is automatically created. However, we have already seen an example where this is not the case. The *input()* function does not always return the data type we want. As a solution, we used the *eval()* function, which evaluates the input and assigns the correct data type.

For beginners, the function is perfectly adequate. Experienced developers, on the other hand, often advise against using it. The reason for this is that the function requires more computing power and runtime than the manual entry of the data type.

Furthermore, the evaluation of the entered expression with the eval() function is sometimes even dangerous. An operator can enter an expression whose evaluation by the function causes damage to the computer on which the programme is running. In practice, eval() is only used when the programme is not operated by anyone other than the programmer.

As an alternative, we can also specify the data types by writing the data type in front of the command to be executed. If we want to save an input as an integer number, we write:

x= int(input("enter a number"))

the number receives the data type *int.*

Type conversion can be applied to all data types.

x= int(input("enter a number")) #int

print(x)

y=float(x) #Conversion to floating point number

print(y)

z=str(y) #Conversion to string

print(z)

We can look at the output at the console.

```
In [10]: runfile('C:/Python_examples/Chapter 3 - Basics/004 Data type conversion.py', wc

enter a number 5
5
5.0
5.0
```

Figure 15Output after type conversion

The second and third output is identical, but the data type *float* has been output 5.0 as a float number and 5.0 as a string. This is also shown by the variable manager in Spyder.

Nan ▲	Type	Size	
x	int	1	5
y	float	1	5.0
z	str	1	5.0

Figure 16Data types after type conversion

3.10. Operators

We have already learned about variables and data types and can not only output the stored values with the *print()* function, but can also calculate with them or compare different variables with each other.

Various **operators** are used for this purpose that can be divided into different classes. Some of the operators are logically understandable, such as the plus and minus signs.

 The operators such as plus, minus, times and divided and others are called **arithmetic** operators.

The following table shows the most common arithmetic operators in Python and their function.

Arithmetic operators

Operator	Meaning	Example	Function
=	Allocation	x=3	
+	Addition	x=y+2	
-	Subtraction	x=y-2	
*	Multiplication	x=y*2	

/	Division	x=y/2	
**	Exponentiation	y=x**3	$y=x^3$
%	Modulo	x = 10%3	Provides the remainder when dividing. 10 divided by 3 gives 3, re-mainder 1, so x takes the value 1.
//	Integer division	x = 10//3	Returns the integer result of a division. 10 divided by 3 gives 3. The remainder is not taken into account.

In addition to the arithmetic operators, which are used for calculation, there are other **operators,** such as the **comparison operators.**

 In contrast to the arithmetic operators, the operation of the compari-son operators is **binary, which** means that there are only two possible results.

There are only two possible answers to the question: "*Is the content of the vari-able x greater than the number five? Either the (un)equation is* **true** *and there-fore true or it is not true and therefore* **false.**

 The result of a comparison can only assume two states - **true** or **false**. If you want to compare two numbers or variables with each other, you therefore need the comparison operators.

The following table still illustrates the use of comparison operators and their re-sult.

Comparison operators

Operator	Meaning	Example	Result
<	Smaller?	3<5	True
<=	Smaller equal?	5<=3	False
>	Bigger?	5>3	True
>=	Bigger equal?	5>=3	True
==	In a moment?	5==4	False

!=	Unequal?	4!=5	True

 The simple (=) equal sign is an **assignment**. If one wants to check whether two variables are equal, two equal signs (==) must be set.

x=5 # The variable x is assigned the value 5

x==5 # It is checked whether x contains the value 5. The result is True or False

The command *print(3<4)* returns "True" as the result.

 Why are there no inverted commas here? What would the console output be if you put them in?

Solution: When inverted commas are used, the text, and not the result of the operation, is output. In the case print("3<4") 3<4 would be output.

The last sub-item we will look at is **logical operators. Logical** operators interpret every numerical value and every variable as true or false, similar to the comparison operators. Every value except zero is interpreted as true. Only the zero is assumed to be false. Logical operators are usually combined with conditions.

The special feature of logical operators is that the operator itself is not a character but a word.

The most important operators are shown in the following table.

Logical operators

Operator	Meaning	Example	Function
Not	Negation	x = not y;	If y is true, x becomes false and vice versa
and	And	x = y and z	If y and z are true, x is true, otherwise x is false
or	Or	x =y or z	If y or z are true, x is true, otherwise x is false

What is the value of the variable z in each case?

$x = 5z$ $= not\ x$	The number 5 is interpreted as "True". Accordingly, the variable z receives the value "False".
$x = 6 ; y = 0z$ $= x\ and\ y$	x is "True", but y is not. Accordingly, the variable z is "False".
$x = 6 ; y = 0z$ $= x\ or\ y$	x is "True", y is "False". It is sufficient if x or y is "True". Therefore z is also "True"
$x = 6 ; y = 0z$ $= x\ and\ not\ y$	x is "True", y is "False". "not y" is therefore "True". Accordingly, the variable z is also "True".

This has given us an overview of the most important components when calculating with variables. Operators and variables are basic building blocks of every programme and are used in many combinations and possibilities. In order to be able to use the operators and variables meaningfully, we will look at how **functions** work in Python in the next subchapter.

3.11. Functions

Some **functions** have already been introduced, for example the print() function, which outputs data to the console. Most people remember functions from school lessons: $y = 2 \cdot x + 1$ is an example of a function.

The basic idea is that we pass a number x to the function and then get a number y back.

 When programming, however, a function is not limited to numbers as input or output values.

For example, you can pass a letter or a whole word to a function instead of a number. The value passed is called an **argument.**

 A function is called by its name followed by two round brackets. The brackets contain the required arguments of the function.

You do not necessarily get a number back either.

As an example, we will again use our well-known function *print().*

The *print()* function can be passed variables, terms or sentences.

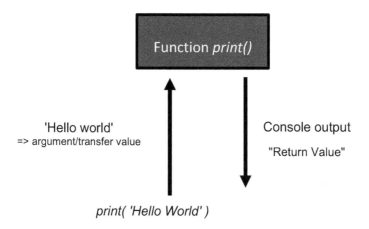

'Hello world'
=> argument/transfer value

Console output

"Return Value"

print('Hello World')

Figure 17 Function call

A console output is triggered as the **return value.**

The *print()* function is just one example of a function, next we will look at other very useful functions.

4. Data storage and processing

4.1. Lists

Python is excellently designed to work with large data sets. However, we quickly reach our limits with simple variables. If we want to store hundreds of numbers, we would have to create hundreds of variables. It makes more sense to store several related variables in one variable. As a solution, a new data type is introduced, the so-called **lists**.

This is, as the name suggests, a list, i.e. a string of words or numbers stored together in a single variable.

The creation of a list is analogous to the creation of a variable, with the difference that square brackets are placed at the beginning and end of the list. This way the interpreter knows that it is a list.

 The elements of the list are separated by commas. For words (*strings*), again the inverted commas must not be forgotten.

dataset = ["Tom", 26, 1.84]

The example creates a list with the three elements and saves the list in the variable *dataset*. The variable now has the data type *list*. Tom stands for the name, 26 for the age and 1.84 for the height.

Normally we would have had to create three separate variables. So, the advantage of lists is obvious.

Using the example, we can also derive other properties.

 As you can quickly see, a list can contain different data types, here *string/str, int* and *float*. Each element of the list automatically receives an **index**, starting at **zero**.

If you want to query individual elements of a list, the index must be written in brackets.

print(dataset[0])	outputs the first element ["Tom"].
print(dataset[2])	outputs the third element [1.84].
print(dataset[:1])	outputs a partial list ["Tom"].
print(dataset[1:2])	outputs a partial list [26, 1.84].

print(dataset[-1])   outputs the last element [1.84].

print(dataset[-2])   outputs the penultimate element [26].

How can we interpret the index **-1** and **-2**? There is no negative list element, is there?

Well, the lists can quickly have many hundreds of items or new items can be added all the time.

If we want to access the **last elements**, we can enter the last index. However, sometimes the index is not known or it is very large. Therefore, in Python, negative indexes can be used to select the last elements appended.

list = [0,1,....,9999999]

#We want to read out the 999,999,999th element

list[9999999]# works

list [-1] #better

Calculating with lists:

Lists can contain elements with different types. However, we can also calculate with the whole list, i.e. the complete "data set" at once. For example, we can add any elements to a list, overwrite them or delete them. As an example, let's take our list with the name, age and height of a person:

dataset = ["Tom", 26, 1.84]

Through the command

dataset[1] = 27

the age is overwritten from 26 to 27.

With the command

del dataset[1]

the element with *index 1 is* completely deleted.

Adding and multiplying

Although lists often contain words or sentences, they can still be added, multiplied or nested. When adding lists, the following must be observed:

 If a single element or a list is added to another list, only the individual elements are appended to the end of the existing list.

```
dataset1 = [ "Tom", 26,1.84]
dataset2 = ["Lisa",28,1.67]
dataset3 = dataset1 + dataset2
print(dataset3)
```

⇨   ['Tom', 26, 1.84, 'Lisa', 28, 1.67]

Individual elements can also be attached.

```
dataset3 = dataset1 + ["new element"]
print(dataset3)
```

⇨   ['Tom', 26, 1.84, 'new item']

 When multiplying by a number n, the existing list is duplicated n times and appended. Example for *n=3*:

```
dataset3 = dataset1*3
print(dataset3)
```

⇨   ['Tom', 26, 1.84, 'Tom', 26, 1.84, 'Tom', 26, 1.84]

Multidimensional lists

Besides words and variables, the elements of a list can themselves be lists. These lists can in turn contain lists as elements and so on and so forth.

These are also referred to as **multidimensional lists**.

To create a multi-dimensional list, we create an ordinary list with square brackets. Then we enter a complete list between the commas. It makes sense not to write all the lists in one line, but to structure them one below the other in several lines. The lines must be indented. Spyder recognises this automatically and indents the lines.

```
dataset4 =[
['Tom', 26,1.84], # First element
['Lisa',28,1.67], # Second element
['Kevin',34,1.78], # Third element
]
```

 If you retrieve individual values from the list, the element is output as usual. This time the element is a whole list, so that the whole list is also output.

print(dataset4[1])

⇨   *['Lisa', 28, 1.67]*

If one wants to query an element of a sub-list, for example *Kevin*, first the index of the sub-list and then the index of the element is given.

In the example, the element *Kevin* is in the third sub-list (index 2) and is in the list again the first element (index 0).

print(datensatz4[2][0])

⇨   *Kevin*

What does the command *print(dataset4[0][1])* output?
The index zero stands for the first sub-list, of which the element with index 1 is "26".

What does the command *print(dataset4[-1][:2])* output?
The index -1 stands for the last sub-list, of which the elements with index zero to 1 (two elements) are
['Kevin', 34].

Next, we will learn other methods to create or edit a list.

The commands are not essential and we can also create the same list manually, but we save a lot of time if we know the right shortcut.

Creating a list with range()

·̣ϙ̣·   The function ***range(x)*** creates a list with the values **zero to x**. The command

list = range(10)

assigns the values [0,1,2,3,4,5,6,7,8,9] to the list.

It must be noted that no element with the data type *list* is created, but an element of the data type *range*. In the context of this book, this is equivalent in its use.

For a console output, a type conversion can take place so that the individual elements are output.

list = range(10) # type range

print("Output as range element:",list)

list2=list(list) #Type conversion to list

print("Output as list element:",list2)

Data storage and processing

```
In [3]: runfile('C:/Python_examples/Chapter 4 - Data storage and processing/001 lists.py', wd:
Output as range element: range(0, 10)
Output as list element: [0, 1, 2, 3, 4, 5, 6, 7, 8, 9]
```

Figure 18 Comparison of range and list

A look at the variable explorer confirms the type conversion.

Nam ▲	Type	Size		Value
list1	range	1	range object	
list2	list	10	[0, 1, 2, 3, 4, 5, 6, 7, 8, 9]	

Help Variable explorer Plots Files

Figure 19 Variable Explorer

Alternatively, the start and end value can also be given to the *range()* function. In this case, the end value is **not** generated!

list = range(3,7)

Passes the values [3,4,5,6] to the list. **Without the seven.**

The function *range()* will be of importance in the next chapter (loops and conditions).

4.2. Edit lists

You can do more than just calculate with lists. There are also functions that simplify the editing of lists considerably.

As lists are a very common and simple tool for data storage, there are many tools to simplify their use, such as **methods**.

Methods are special functions that cannot be used for all data. The exact difference is explained in the chapter *Classes,* as this is not necessary for the present understanding and application.

With the *del* command for deleting a list, a method has already been introduced, but not marked as such.

In addition, there are many other methods for editing a list. For this it is important to know the method names.

 To add another element to the end of a list, this is possible with the **append() command.**

list.append('Element')

The name of the list is called followed by a dot and the method name.The element that is passed to the method is appended to the end of the list "liste":

dataset1 = ['Tom', 26,1.84]

dataset1.append('Football')

The fourth element in the example is *football* and is added to the list *"dataset1"*.

In addition, there are other methods for use with the data type list.

For example, individual elements can be searched for or deleted. The **index()** command is used to search for an element.

listname.index('Element')

#searches for an element and returns the index.

An element, for example a word, is passed to the method. The list is then searched and the index of the matching element is then output as the return value of the *index()* method.

print(dataset1.index('Tom'))

returns the value 0 at the console, since *Tom* is the element with index zero.

The following table shows the most common methods for use in conjunction with lists.

.append()	Adds an item to the end of the list.
.clear()	Deletes all elements of the list
.copy()	Creates a copy of the list
.count()	Returns the number of existing entries within the list
.extend()	Appends all elements of a second list.
.index()	Returns the index of a searched element. If not available: *list1=list(range(10))* *list1.index(11)* *ValueError: 11 is not in list*

.insert()	Adds an element to the list. The index and the element to which the element is to be added are passed. All other elements move one position backwards.
.pop()	Deletes an element from the list. The return value is the deleted value.
.remove()	Deletes an element from the list. list1=list(range(10)) list1.remove(5)
.sort()	Sorts the list by value, either in ascending order (numbers) or alphabetically (strings).
reverse()	Mirrors all values of a list, the last value becomes the first, and vice versa.

Furthermore, there are operators that can be applied to lists. We can compare these operators with the +,-* and / operators that we can apply to numbers.

The following table shows the calls and function of the operators

x in list	Returns True if the element x occurs in the list. Otherwise False
x not in list	Returns "False" if the element x occurs in the list, otherwise "True".
len(list)	Outputs the length (number of elements) of the list.
min(list)	Returns the smallest element.
max(list)	Returns the largest element.
sum(list)	Returns the sum of the list.

Lists are a simple and widespread way to store related, variable data. Lists make it easy to calculate and use different methods. Tuples are a similar way of storing data.

4.3. Tuple

Lists always contain variable data, which makes working with them very convenient, but this variable data also occupies additional memory. In addition, more memory must always be kept free than is initially needed if the variable changes and becomes larger.

However, if we only have unchanging values, we use so-called **tuples** instead of lists. Tuples behave very similarly to lists. However, the values of the elements cannot be changed. To create a tuple, the square brackets of the list are omitted. The commas still separate the elements from each other.

```
tuple = "Tom", 26, 1.84
```

The elements can be retrieved by naming the index, as with lists.

```
print(tuple[0]) # outputs Tom.
```

However, you cannot overwrite or delete the values.

For example, if you want to delete an element with the *del command*, an error is output that the tuples do not support this command.

```
del tuple[2]
```

Deletion is not possible.

However, further elements can be added. For this purpose, as with lists, the plus sign is used.

Note, however, that no list or words can be added to a tuple, only another tuple.

```
tuple1 = 'Tom', 26, 1.84
```

```
tuple2 = 'male', 'football
```

```
tuple3 = tuple1+tuple2
```

As always, it depends on the concrete application whether lists or tuples are to be preferred. This also brings us to the third, very similar type of data storage, dictionaries. These are also extremely useful for certain applications.

4.4. Dictionaries

After the handling of lists and tuples has been explained, another very similar variant for data structuring is discussed below: **dictionaries.**

We are now familiar with lists. The big disadvantage of lists is that the user has to know what each index stands for.

In the example of our data set of *Tom, it* was determined that index 0 stands for the name, index 1 for the age and index 2 for the height.

```
dataset1 = ['Tom',26,1.84]
```

It would be much cleverer if you could specify a search term instead of an index. For example, instead of the index "zero" the search term *name*

Dictionaries were created to solve this problem. They are structured very similarly to a list, but meet our requirements and translate the index into a search term (**key**).

 Dictionaries contain keys and **values**. The keys are usually character strings.

As an example, we create the same person file again. The keys and values are written in curly brackets and assigned to each other by means of a colon. The value pairs are separated with commas.

person1= {'name':'Tom','age':'26','height':'1,84'}

Here, name, age and height are the keys and Tom, 26 and 1.84 are the values.

 Instead of specifying the index (as with lists), the desired value can be retrieved via the key.

print(person1['name'])

print(person1['age'])

```
In [6]: runfile('C:/Python_examples/Chapter 4 - Data storage and processing/002 Dictionary
Tom
26
```

Figure 20 Output of values

The use of the dictionaries is appropriate because of the **logical connection between** the keys and the values.

There are also many help functions for dictionaries. As with lists, you can delete, append or insert certain elements.

With ***person1.keys()*** all keys can be output.

 With ***person1.values()*** all values can be output.

With ***person1.items()*** all contained keys and the corresponding values can be output.

```
In [7]: runfile('C:/Python_examples/Chapter 4 - Data storage and processing/002
dict_keys(['name', 'age', 'height'])
dict_values(['Tom', '26', '1,84'])
dict_items([('name', 'Tom'), ('age', '26'), ('height', '1,84')])
```

Figure 21 Text output person1.items()

4.5. Loops and conditions

 Loops and conditions are auxiliary tools for controlling a programme more clearly and efficiently. Loops can be used to **repeat** certain sections of the programme.

Conditions can be used to **skip** or execute parts of the programme under certain programme conditions. This enables the programme to respond to different events with different reactions.

 One of the most important statements for programming is the *if-condition*. It is present in almost all programming languages and is an essential tool with many possibilities.

4.6. if- condition

 The "if-then" statement is only executed if a condition is fulfilled. The condition is stated after the signal word "*if*". The word "then" is replaced by a colon, so to speak.

if x > 4 :

It is important to understand that the condition is "checked for truth". If you notice that you still have problems understanding how to interpret "True/False" statements, you should take another look at the operator table in the chapter on *operators*.

 All instructions that are executed when the condition is fulfilled are **indented in** the line when writing. This can be realised by the tab key or several spaces. In any case, it should be kept consistent.

Correct - indented	Wrong - not indented
if x > 4 :	*if x > 4 :*
print("The number is greater than 4")	*print("The number is greater than 4")*

 If the condition is met, the indented programme code is executed.

If the condition is not met, the *if statement is* skipped and the programme continues after the indented text.

If we want to integrate alternative statements to be executed when the condition is not met, we use the ***else command***.

If we want to query not only two but several conditions, this works with the extension **elif** (abbreviation for else-if). We can insert as many *elif scenarios as we like,* but only one *if-* and one *else-scenario.*

Else and *elif* are optional with an *if statement*:

```
temp1 = eval(input('Enter temperature')) A variable is read in

if temp1==20:      #If temp1 has the value 20

   print('The temperature is 20 °C')

elif temp1 == 25:   #If temp1 has the value 25

   print('The temperature is 25 °C')

elif temp1 == 30:   #If temp1 has the value 30

   print('The temperature is 30 °C')

else:               #In all other cases

   print('The temperature is neither 20, nor 25, nor 30 °C')
```

The *if-condition* can also be used in conjunction with a string.

```
x='hello

if x == 'hello':

   print(" Hello World") # if the var. x contains the character string "Hello".

else:

   print("Bye")
```

 The *if-condition* needs a true statement to be executed. We can realise this, as in the example above, through a query. Alternatively, a variable that already has a Boolean value (True/False) is sufficient.

```
x = True

if x:

   print("x is true")

else:

   print("x is wrong")
```

In the example, x is set to "True", therefore "*x is true*" is output.

 If no comparison operator is used, any number other than zero is interpreted as *true.* Only zero itself is interpreted as *false.*

```
x = 3 # 3 is interpreted as True

if x:
```

print('x is true')

else:

print('x is wrong')

⇨   *"x is true"*

 Check for yourself: When is the *if-condition* fulfilled and when is it not?

If 3 > 5 :

if 3 < 5 :

if 3 :

if 0 :

if not 3 :

if 2==2 :

if (4>2) && (3<1) :

Solution:

1. *Not fulfilled. Since 3 is less than 5, the if statement is not executed.*

2. *Met. 3 is less than 5, therefore the if statement is executed.*

3. *Met. 3 is a non-zero number, so it is interpreted as "true" and the if statement is executed.*

4. *Not fulfilled. The number zero is interpreted as "false" and the if statement is not executed.*

5. *Not fulfilled. The number three is interpreted as true but negated, therefore the if statement is not executed.*

6. *Fulfilled, because 2==2 is a true result.*

 Attention, here "==" must be used to check a true statement. The operator "=" is an assignment, not a check. If 2=2 would result in an error (invalid syntax). A common error!

7. *Not fulfilled. Since both 4 would have to be greater than 2 and 3 less than 1, the if statement is not executed.*

4.7. While loop

Loops are needed to repeatedly execute computing operations. This can be timed, for example when you want to measure the room temperature every 15 minutes, or within fractions of a second, for example when an artificial intelligence solves individual mathematical tasks.

The structure of the while loop is analogous to the if operation. The while loop is introduced by the key term while. The condition is then specified. After that, it is concluded with a colon.

The commands to be executed are again indented.

```
while temp1 > 20:
        print("The temperature is greater than 20 °C")
```

At first, there is no difference to the if-query. However, an if-query asks only once whether the operation is fulfilled.

 A while loop keeps running until the condition becomes *"false"*. The loop can also run indefinitely if the condition is always logically *fulfilled*.

 If the operation to be checked is not changed within the While loop, it continues to run indefinitely.

This is also the case in the following example. The variable *temp1* is not changed. If the variable is greater than 20, there would be an infinite loop.

We can stop the loop with **STRG+C.**

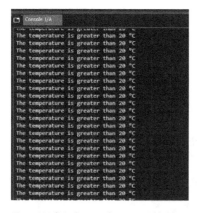

Figure 22 Infinite loop, as the test variable is never changed

This can be remedied, for example, by changing the variable **within the loop.**

```
while temp1 > 20:

    print('The temperature is greater than 20 °C')

    temp1= eval(input('How many degrees is it at the moment?'))
```

In this example, the user is prompted within the loop to enter a new temperature. If the entered temperature is 20 °C or lower, the loop will not be run again during the next query. A **count variable** is often used in conjunction with a While loop. This is a variable, usually *i, ii or j*, which is incremented by one per run. With the help of the count variable, the number of runs can be recorded and a termination condition can be introduced, for example, if the count variable rises above a certain value, the loop is terminated.

```
i =1#      Count variable

while i < 10: # There should be a total of 9 runs (1-9)

  print("Pass number:",i)

  i=i+1
```

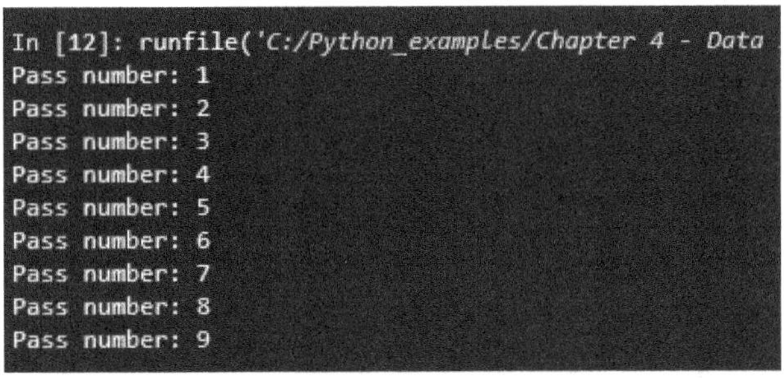

```
In [12]: runfile('C:/Python_examples/Chapter 4 - Data
Pass number: 1
Pass number: 2
Pass number: 3
Pass number: 4
Pass number: 5
Pass number: 6
Pass number: 7
Pass number: 8
Pass number: 9
```

Figure 23 The loop is run through 9 times

4.8. The for loop

In principle, you can replace a **for loop** with a while loop and vice versa. However, depending on the task, it makes sense to use the appropriate loop type.

For-loops are mainly used in combination with **lists** and other objects that contain **several elements.** Each element is checked. As soon as the for-loop cannot find any more suitable elements, the loop is aborted. The structure is again analogous to the if-query and the while-loop.

```
car_brands = ['VW','Audi','Porsche','BMW','Skoda']
```

```
for x in car_brands:        # As long as an element is present

    print(x)                # It is output
```

In the for loop, the signal word is for. Then we specify any variable. This is followed by the signal word **in** and the list or sequence of elements.

As long as an element is present, the condition is fulfilled. The element of the list is stored in the variable *x*. In the subsequent run, the next element is checked. The output looks as follows:

```
In [14]: runfile('C:/Python_examples/Chapter 4 - Data s
VW
Audi
Porsche
BMW
Skoda
```

Figure 24 Output of all list items

If a loop is to complete a certain number of runs, a suitable list can be created with the help of the function **range()**.

```
for n in range(10): # 10 passes with the elements 0-9

    print (n)
```

```
In [15]: runfile('C:/Python_examples/Chapter 4 - Data stor
0
1
2
3
4
5
6
7
8
9
```

Figure 25Output of the list range(10)

The function *range(10)* creates a list from zero to the specified number [0,1,2,3,4,5,6,7,8,9]. The specified number is excluded.

This list is passed to the for loop. The for loop works through the elements. Therefore, a total of 10 passes (0-9) take place.

4.9. Cancel with break()

We learned how to use loops and conditions and how to intercept different cases.

Often, however, we do not want to execute a loop completely, but terminate it prematurely.

The simplest example is a search algorithm. It runs through a list until it finds the matching element.

After that, however, it should not continue searching, but cancel the loop.

 The termination of a loop, function or condition can be realised with the signal word *break.* As soon as this appears within a loop, it is aborted.

```
Car_brands = ['VW','Audi','Porsche','BMW','Skoda']

search = input('Which brand should be searched for? \n')

print("start searching")

for n in car_brands:

    if n == search: # If the matching element was found

        print('The brand was found')

        break                # Loop is aborted

    print(n)                 #Otherwise the mark is output
```

First, the list *car_brands is* created and passed to the for loop. The loop compares the current element of the list with the desired input. If there is a hit (if n == search), the for loop is aborted. Otherwise, it continues to run and outputs all elements of the list.

```
In [21]: runfile('C:/Python_examples/Chapter 4 - Data

Which brand should be searched for?
Porsche
start searching
VW
Audi
The brand was found
```

Figure 26 Car_brands – start searching

4.10. Exercise - Lists and Dictionaries

We have covered the basics such as variables, operators and lists. We can also make decisions with the help of if statements. In general, the structure of loops in Python is kept very simple. However, errors such as syntax errors, character errors or logical errors inevitably occur at the beginning. That is why it is important that we apply what we have learned and jump straight into the first smaller exercise task.

All required functions and methods have already been covered and can be looked up if needed.

First exercise

The programmer is to create a programme for a fruit shop warehouse. For the example, we have limited ourselves to only four fruits. The principle remains the same for 100 fruits. Only the programming effort is higher.

There are a total of four different fruits in the warehouse and the corresponding stocks, which are shown in the following table:

Fruit	Stock
Banana	501
Apples	112
Mango	52
Kiwi	96

First, the stocks are to be saved. A list or a dictionary is recommended for this. In the case of a list, implement the query with the *input()* function and the selection of the stock via if and elif statements.

The user should then be asked to enter one of the fruits. The programme should then output the matching stock.

4.11. Solution

As with most programming tasks, there is no model solution here. Every programmer has his or her preferences. One prefers to work with lists, another with dictionaries. One programmer prefers for-loops, another while-loops.

Therefore, besides the following code, there are many different possible solutions for the described task. If the programme gives the desired result with the execution, the code is correct.

 ! When entering the fruit, the respective name must be written in inverted commas, e.g. "banana".

```
'''Stock Exercise'''

''' WITH LISTEN '''

stock = [501,112,52,96] # List with the stock

print("Please enter the desired fruit")

x=input() # The desired fruit must be entered

if x == "banana": # If banana was entered

    index=0 # the index is set to zero

elif x == "apples":

    index=1

elif x == "mango":

    index=2

elif x == "kiwi":

    index=3
```

First, we create the list. Then the user is asked to enter the fruit he is looking for. Since the list only works with indexes, the fruit must be converted to the appropriate index. An if-query is used for this.

The same task becomes much easier when using dictionaries.

```
'''WITH DICTIONARIES'''

stock = {'banana':501,'apples':112,'mango':52,'kiwi':96 }

print("Please enter the desired fruit")

# The fruit corresponds to the index and does not have to be converted

Index=input() # The desired fruit must be entered
```

 We can quickly see that for this example, the use of dictionaries offers a clear advantage. The function is the same.

```
# The stock is then output

print("There are still",stock[index], "pieces", x, "available")
```

or for the Dictionary variant:

print("There are still",stock[index], "pieces", index, "available")

#with both variants, the stock is finally output.

The last *print() command is a* little more complex. First, the string ("There are still") is output.

The element then appears with the index that was previously defined.

After that, the previously queried fruit, which was stored in *x* or *index,* is output. At last, the string *present* is displayed. In sum, the execution of the programme looks like this:

```
In [27]: runfile('C:/Python_examples/Examples/Cap 4- fruits_
Please enter the desired fruit

mango
There are still 52 pieces mango available
```

Figure 26 Output Exercise Lists and Dictionaries

Congratulations, we have written our first programme.
Of course, it is very minimalistic. You couldn't sell it to a customer like that yet and certainly not everything worked straight away, but: practice makes perfect! Even experienced programmers often get error messages or not everything works as it should right away. With time, the notations become more familiar and you no longer have to look up the standard commands like *print()* or *input()* every time.
This brings us to the next big topic. We know several standard functions by now, in the following chapter we will create our own functions.

4.12. Create functions yourself

We have already learned what functions are and what they are used for in the chapter *Functions.*

We can call a function by passing it one or more arguments.

Within the function, commands are then processed and as a result we receive (not necessarily) one or more return values. Even though many standard functions already exist, it sometimes happens that we need a function that has not been created before. Therefore, it is useful and helpful to be able to write functions yourself.

Our own functions are useful when we use parts of a programme more often.

A self-created function is written into the same file as the main pro-gramme. The signal word here is **def,** followed by the name of the func-tion.

The same rules apply to the naming as to the assignment of variable names. Here, too, it is advantageous to assign a name that directly indicates the purpose of the function.

For the following sections, a function is created to which a number x *is* passed. The return value is to be $y=x^2$. Python has the ** operator for this purpose, but in this example the command is to be realised with a function. A sensible name for the function would be, for example, *xsquare (x)*

def xsquare(x):

 After specifying the name of the function, round brackets are set. A transfer value (an argument) can be written in these.

For the *xsquare* function, this is a number x. We will create this later in the main programme.

Then, as with the *if-query* and loops, a colon is placed. The commands must also be indented here. We see that there are recurring formatting patterns in Python.

The transferred variable x can be used within the programme. Any commands can be executed.

def xsquare(x):

    y=x*x

    print(x,"-square is ",y)

 The transfer value can also be empty, for example with the already known function *input()*. This does not necessarily require a transfer value.

After we have created the function, we can call the function. For the example, the number three is passed, i.e. the function is **called**.

def xsquare(x):

    y=x*x

    print(x,'- square is',y)

xsquare(3)   # The number three is passed to the function.

 The call to the function must no longer be indented, otherwise this line belongs to the function and not to the main programme. The colons are also omitted from the call.

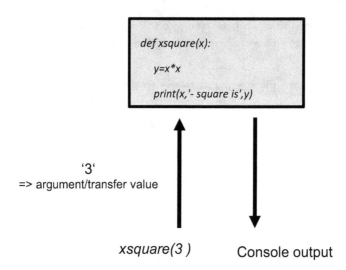

```
def xsquare(x):

    y=x*x

    print(x,'- square is',y)
```

'3'
=> argument/transfer value

xsquare(3)   Console output

Figure 27Function call xsquare(3)

As output we receive:

```
In [30]: runfile('C:/Python_examples/Chapter 4 - [
3  squared is  9
```

Figure 28Output of the function call

Next, we want to execute the *print() command in* the main programme and no longer within the function. For this, the *print() command is* no longer indented. This means that it is no longer part of the function.

It must also be written after the function call.

```
def xsquare(x):

        y=x*x

xsquare(3)

print(x,'- square is',y)
```

Actually, the same output should occur, shouldn't it?

However, this programme code gives the following error message:

```
In [31]: runfile('C:/Python_examples/Chapter 4 - Data st
Traceback (most recent call last):

  File "C:\Python_examples\Chapter 4 - Data storage and
    print(x," squared is ",y)

NameError: name 'x' is not defined
```

Figure 29 Error message name 'x' is not defined

But why? After all, the variable *x is* used in the function. To do this, we need to look at the difference between **local** and **global** variables.

When creating functions, it is important to understand that the variables x and y cannot be used outside the programme. They are restricted to the function and can only be used within it. They are therefore also called local variables.

Python, like many other programming languages, distinguishes between local variables, which are created within a function, and global variables, which can be used in the main programme. This has the advantage, for example, that local variables can be deleted again after use, so that no unnecessary memory is occupied.

A function forms a **black box, so** to speak, to which a value can be passed. The values inside the black box can be viewed, but not used outside the box.

 If one wants to use the value of a variable from a function, it must be returned with the command ***return.***

Returned means that the function call is replaced by the return value. As an example, we know the *input() command.*

input('Please enter a number')

The command prompts the user to enter a string. The return value is the string entered. If we want to save the return value, we have to store it in a variable.

input= input('Please enter a number')

Here again it is important to understand that only **a value** is returned and not the **local variable** itself. Local means that we cannot access it outside the function.

If we remember the Box model for variables, it is the content of the variable that is returned, not the variable itself.

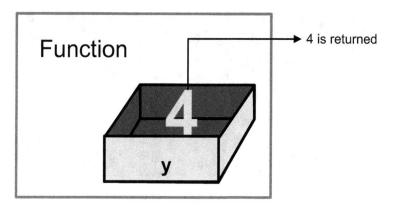

Figure 30 *Function return values in the box model*

However, the returned value can be stored in another **global variable**. This can be used in the main programme as well as in the functions.

For the global variable, even the same name of the local variable can be used, because the local variable does not exist outside the function.

As an example, we apply the *return command to the xsquare()* function:

```
def xsquare(x):
        y = x*x#          Local variable y
        return y#         The value of y is returned
x = 3                 # x is defined
y = xsquare(x)        # y is assigned the return value
print(x,'- square is',y)
```

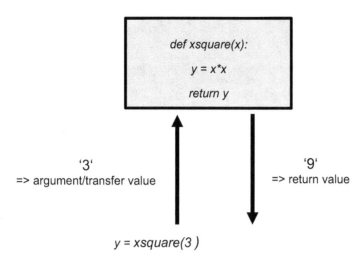

 replaced — see below.

$$def\ xsquare(x):$$

$$y = x^*x$$

$$return\ y$$

'3'
=> argument/transfer value

'9'
=> return value

$$y = xsquare(3\ )$$

Figure 31Function xsquare with return command

We see that the local variable *y is* assigned the value *x*x*, which is then returned as the value of y. The variable y cannot be used outside the function. The variable y cannot be used outside the function.

The example can be written even more compactly by omitting the "diversions" via the local variable *y. Instead, x*x is returned directly.* Instead, *x*x* is returned directly. In Python, the mathematical expression *x*x* is first calculated and the result returned.

```
def xsquare(x):
    return x*x#   x*x is calculated, then the value is returned
```

 If a function returns values with the help of the *return command*, the function is also automatically terminated. Therefore, the *return command* must always be the last command of the function.

Several *return commands* are also possible, for example within an if statement.

For this, let's look at another example where the return command is used.

A temperature value is passed to the following function.

```
def weather(temp):        # temp is transferred
    if temp > 30:
        return "It's too warm"
    elif temp < 15:
        return "It's too cold"
    else:
```

```
    return "It is pleasant"
''' Main Programme'''
x= eval(input("How many degrees is it? \n"))    #User input
y = weather(x)                # The return string is stored in y
print(y)                      # And then output
```

We see that return values are not limited to numbers. Strings are also possible. However, the return value depends on whether the if statement is fulfilled or not.

Depending on which case occurs, different strings are returned.

4.13. Set standard arguments

So far, we have learned about functions that we can call by passing the appropriate arguments. In the chapter on *console output with print()* we programmed an empty line by not setting an argument.

```
print() # Outputs an empty line
```

In this case, no argument is passed. This is possible because the function does not expect an argument or by setting **default values** within a function in case no argument is given. With the help of default values, a function and its call can be simplified. Complex functions sometimes have several arguments that are "reserved" for special cases. For these, many default values are set.

 When you create a function, you can assign default values to the arguments. If no value is passed when the function is called, the default value is taken. If a value is passed, the default value is overwritten.

As an example, we extend the function *xsquare()* so that every power can be calculated. The function thus calculates the term

x to the power of n $y = x^n$

The function requires **two arguments**, the base *x* and the exponent *n*.

```
def x_power_n(x,n):
  y = x**n
 return y
```

Next, we want to set n to 2 by default, i.e. if you only pass x, n will get the value 2. For this, we set *n=2* when defining the function.

```
def x_power_n(x,n=2):

    y = x**n

return y
```

We call the function, passing only one value. This is assigned to the local variable x in the function.

The function call

```
print(x_poower_n(3)) # x=3 n=2 (default)
```

consequently outputs 9, since $3^2 = 9$

On the other hand, if the value for n is also passed, the default value of 2 is over-written.

```
print(x_power_n(3,3)) # x=3 , n=3
```

spends 27, as $3^3 = 27$

We have to make sure that all arguments with default values are at **the end of the input**.

Why this is so can be easily explained with the example:

```
def x_power_n(x=5,n):
```

Here x is set as 5. Now it would be assumed that if we only pass a number, the number will automatically be assigned to the variable n. However, this is not always the case.

The call

```
print(x_power_n(3))        # x =3 , n = undefined
```

overwrites the variable **x** to 3, as this comes **before** the n.

Since no further value for n was specified afterwards, an error message appears that too few arguments have been passed.

```
SyntaxError: non-default argument follows default argument.
```

```
'Argument without default value follows an argument with default value'.
```

To avoid this, this error is automatically detected and the error message appears even before the function is executed.

4.14. Outsource functions in modules

We already know how to apply functions and even how to programme functions ourselves. We pass one or more arguments to these functions and receive one or more return values if necessary.

The functions dealt with were relatively simple in structure. The *xsquare()* function consists of only a few lines.

More complex functions, on the other hand, can take up significantly more lines of code. In addition, with larger programmes, dozens to hundreds of functions can be used quickly. It therefore makes sense to save the creation of functions in a separate file.

These only appear in the main programme when they are called up. This procedure optimises the overview and structure of the programme.

In addition, a programmer can pass on his own created functions to other programmers without them having to receive the entire main programme. An example is the function *print()*. Its programme code has not yet appeared anywhere, yet we use it without any problems.

To outsource a function ourselves, we create a new file in which we write all the functions we want to outsource. This is saved as *modul_xsquare.py.*

A file that contains outsourced functions is called a **module.**

As an example of a module, the *xsquare()* function is written in the file *modul_xsquare.py.*

```
C:\Python_examples\Chapter 4 - Data storage and processing\module\modul_xsquare.py
   modul_xsquare.py
1    def xsquare(x):
2        y=x*x
3        print(x," squared is ",y)
4        return y
```

Figure 32 The function has been outsourced to a module

In the example, the module contains only one function. Usually, several functions are combined in one module.

The next step is to create the main programme. This could look like the following:

```
x = eval(input("Enter a number \n")) # x is defined

y = xsquare(x)      # y is assigned the return value

print(x,'- square is',y)
```

The programme asks the user to enter a number. The xsquare() function is then called, which returns the square of the number entered. The number and the square are output for the console. Before we can use the module, we have to import it with the signal word import. The extension .py of the file is omitted.

```
import module_xsquare
```

The module has been imported, but the *xsquare()* function cannot be used without adaptation. In order to be able to use the function from the module, first the module name, then a dot and then the function name is written when calling the function.

```
import module_xsquare

x = eval(input("Enter a number \n"))  # x is defined

y =module_xsquare.xsquare(x)

print(x,'- square is',y)
```

 It must be ensured that the module and the main programme are in the same folder.

Alternatively, a subfolder can be created. In this case, the path of the sub-folder must also be prefixed when importing the module. The same applies to the function call; here, too, the path of the subfolder must be prefixed.

 If the file *module_xsquare is* in the subfolder *module,* then the subfolder is written in front of the module with a dot as a separator.

```
import module.module_xsquare

y= module.module_xsquare.xsquare(x)
```

Depending on the location of the function, we need to specify a module and possibly a subfolder.

y = xsquare(x)	If the function is listed in the same programme
import module_xsquare *y =module_xsquare.xsquare(x)*	If the function in the file modul_xsqare is in the same folder
import module.module_xsquare *y= module.module_xsquare.xsquare(x)*	If the file module_xsquare is in the subfolder module

It is obvious that especially the third variant quickly becomes confusing. The name of the saved module module_xsquare is not advantageously chosen. The module name must be written in front of each function call. This makes the function calls long and confusing.

Alternatively, a module can be imported once into the main programme in order to subsequently assign a function of the module to a function in the main programme. The same name as the function is used for this.

Function = Subfolder.Module.Function_from_the_Module

For the example, it looks like this:

import module.module_xsquare

xsquare = module.module_xsquare.xsquare

Afterwards, the newly created function *xsquare()* which is similar to the function *xsquare() from the* module *modul_xsquare* can be used in the main programme without having to specify the entire path name each time.

import module.module_xsquare

xsquare = module.module_xsquare.xsquare

x=eval(input("Enter a number n"))

y= xsquare(x)   # No path needs to be specified

print(x,'- square is',y)

The advantage of this approach is that one does not have to specify the entire module path each time. However, when programming, the origin of the function is easily overlooked, as it is no longer recognisable from the structure that it was imported from a module.

Another method, which offers a compromise between scope and overview, is to abbreviate the module name when importing.

When one or more modules are imported, one can assign an abbreviation to them. This is done by adding the designation "**as**" after the module name and the chosen abbreviation. This information can be freely chosen. Again, dots serve as separators.

```
import modul_xsquare as xsq
```

From now on, when calling a function, the full module name including the path no longer has to be given, but only the abbreviation.

```
y= xsq.xsquare(x)   # No path needs to be specified
```

It has already been mentioned that one advantage of modules is that they can be passed on independently of the main programme.

It therefore makes sense to use modules that have already been created and not to write them yourself.

Here again, an advantage of Python becomes clear. There is an enormous community around this programming language. Therefore, many standard modules and functions have already been programmed and are freely available to everyone.

If several modules are bundled, this is also called a library.

4.15. Libraries

Libraries are an advantage of the open-source concept that Python follows.

There are many standard libraries that make programming with Python easier. Especially for beginners, it is a good idea to use existing libraries.

For this, however, we need to know exactly how to find the right functions and how to implement them correctly.

A library usually conceals extensive codes, but it is not necessary to understand them in order to use them. Functions such as *input()* or *print()* can be used without importing the associated module, as these **are** so-called **built-in functions**. These are used so frequently that they are built directly into the interpreter. The built-in functions are listed and explained at ***https://docs.python.org/3/library/functions.html***.

Translation:

The Python interpreter has functions and types that are included by default and are therefore always available. They are listed alphabetically in the following table.

Built-in Functions

The Python interpreter has a number of functions and types built into it that are always available. They are listed here in alphabetical order.

Built-in Functions				
abs()	delattr()	hash()	memoryview()	set()
all()	dict()	help()	min()	setattr()
any()	dir()	hex()	next()	slice()
ascii()	divmod()	id()	object()	sorted()
bin()	enumerate()	input()	oct()	staticmethod()
bool()	eval()	int()	open()	str()
breakpoint()	exec()	isinstance()	ord()	sum()
bytearray()	filter()	issubclass()	pow()	super()
bytes()	float()	iter()	print()	tuple()
callable()	format()	len()	property()	type()
chr()	frozenset()	list()	range()	vars()
classmethod()	getattr()	locals()	repr()	zip()
compile()	globals()	map()	reversed()	__import__()
complex()	hasattr()	max()	round()	

Figure 33 Overview of all Built-in Functions

We also find the familiar functions like *input(), eval(), print() or range()* here again.

The standard Python libraries also consist for the most part of normal modules, as explained in the previous chapter. If possible, one should always use these libraries, as this can save a lot of work.

In addition to built-in libraries, Python also uses **built-in constants** such as *True/False* or built-in types such as lists and dictionaries.

 These built-in elements simplify programming and the introduction to Python, even for newcomers.

The standard libraries or the functions they contain are listed under

https://docs.python.org/3/library/index.html. It is advisable to always look up a project first to see if a suitable function or entire modules are already available.

Alternatively, you can usually find the right function for your project within a short time using the search function within the Python page or via the search engines.

4.16. Exercise - Calculate average grade

In the next exercise, we want to consolidate the use of functions. For this purpose, we will create our own function and include it in the main programme.

The following programme is designed to calculate and output a student's average grade.

The average grade is made up of the individual subjects divided by the number of subjects. We assume a simplified case with only three main subjects (Maths, German, English). In this case, the grade results from:

$$\text{Note}_\emptyset = \frac{N_{Ma} + N_{DE} + N_{Eng}}{3}$$

The individual grades of the subjects must first be calculated.

For each subject there is an oral mark and a written mark, which is weighted twice. Thus, for example, the maths grade can be calculated as follows:

$$N_{Ma} = \frac{N_{Ma-mouth} + 2 \cdot N_{Ma-font}}{3}$$

The marks for the exercise are already listed in the following table.
Maths_s corresponds to the written maths mark, Maths_m to the oral mark.

Subject	Maths_s	Math_m	German_s	German_m	English_s	English_m
Mark	1,3	2,0	2,5	2,0	3,0	2,5

 This kind of grading is very Germany-specific. A more internationally version would be to use A-F. But it's more difficult to calculate with letters.

Our assignment for the exercise task is here:
- Save the notes in a list or a dictionary.

- Create a function that calculates the average grade of a subject.

- Then create a function that calculates the average grade of the student.

- Pass the grades of the individual subjects to the functions so that the grades of the subjects and the overall grade are returned.

- Give both the marks of the subjects and the overall mark.

- **Addendum**: Save the functions in a separate file and include them via an import command.

4.17. Solution

As always, there are several possible solutions. The following programme shows only one possible way.
First, we save the grades from the table in a dictionary. The *keys of* the dictionary are the names of the subjects.

```
notes = {'ma_f':1.3,'ma_m':2,
    'de_f':2.5,'de_m':2,
    'en_f':3,'en_m':2.5
    }
```

Then we create a function that calculates and returns the average grade of each subject.

```
def noteSubject(font,mouth):
    return (2*font+mouth)/3
```

Two values are passed to the function. The return value is the average grade of the subject.

For example, if we want to determine the maths grade, we call the *noteFach()* function and pass the corresponding grades from the dictionary.
To obtain the value of the written maths grade (1.3), the key is specified

```
notes['ma_f']
```

Similarly, the value *noten['ma_m']* is called for the oral maths grade (2.0).

```
ma_tot= noteSubject(notes['ma_f'],notes['ma_m'])
```

It makes sense to round the grade to a maximum of two decimal places. The function call is thereby extended to:

```
ma_tot=round(noteSubject(notes['ma_f'],notes['ma_m']),2)
```

Similarly, we call up the function for all subjects.

```
de_tot=round(noteSubject(notes['de_f'],notes['de_m']),2)
```

```
en_tot=round(noteSubject(notes['en_f'],notes['en_m']),2)
```

Thus we have stored the three grades of the subjects in the variables *ma_tot, de_tot and en_tot*.
Then the function for determining the average grade of the three subjects can be created.
The function is named *noteGes()* and three subjects are generally passed to it.

```
def noteTot(subject1,subject2,subject3):
```

```
return (subject1+subject2+subject3)/3
```

After the definition, the function is called. To do this, we pass it the three previously calculated average grades of the subjects. At the same time, we round the grade to two decimal places.

```
n_tot=round(noteTot(ma_tot,de_tot,en_tot),2)
```

The last thing we do is output all the values to the console.

```
print("The overall grade in maths is:",ma_tot)
```

```
print("The overall mark in German is:",de_tot)
```

```
print("The overall grade in English is:",en_tot)
```

```
print("The total score is:",n_tot)
```

Addition:
The two functions *noteSubject()* and *noteTot()* are saved in a module called *modul_noten.py*. The file is in the same folder as the main programme.
In order to be able to use the functions again, we have to use the module in the main programme.

```
import module_notes
```

 Then we have to adapt the function calls. The module is written in front of each function.

```
ma_tot= module_notes.noteSubject(notes['ma_s'],notes['ma_m'])
```

We remember that there is a better alternative than specifying the whole path for each function call. Instead, we reassign the function after importing.

```
import module_notes
```

```
noteSubject = module_notes.noteSubject
```

```
noteGes = module_notes.noteGes
```

This saves us having to specify the module for each function call. With this code, the task was solved and with the help of the tricks we use, it only takes a few lines.
With this programme, the effort is still limited, but it can quickly become confusing for more complex tasks.
Therefore, it is advisable to get used to the procedure described here from the beginning. In the next chapter we will get to know a core element of Python programming, object-oriented programming.

5. Object-Oriented Programming OOP

We have already learned about all the important basic building blocks as well as data storage and data processing. In this chapter, we will look at a technique that we can use to transfer real-life objects into a programme code. To do this, we will first look at the **classification of** objects.

5.1. Classes

Classifying objects from the real world helps our brain to work more effectively. Within fractions of a second, it recognises similarities and differences.

 Classes are used to describe objects or persons (**objects**) with several properties.

A class is an abstract term that describes the commonalities in the behaviour of objects. This is referred to as classification. Let's take the class *human as an* example.

The class *human being* can be defined, for example, with the attributes *name, age, height* etc. and show different behaviours (*speaking, working, sleeping* etc.). Each individual human being is an **object of** the class.

 For this reason, programming with classes is also called **object-oriented programming, or OOP for** short. An object describes the representation of a real object (the human being) from the "real world".

With the help of the class, you can create any number of objects (people) that all have the same **attributes.**

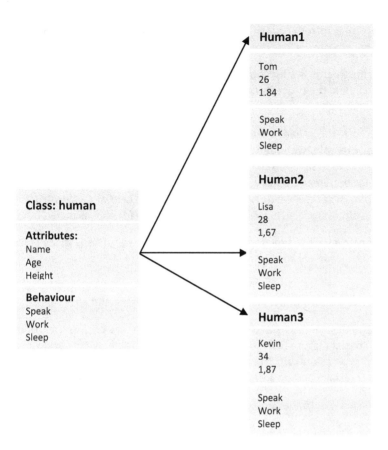

Human1

Tom
26
1.84

Speak
Work
Sleep

Human2

Lisa
28
1,67

Speak
Work
Sleep

Human3

Kevin
34
1,87

Speak
Work
Sleep

Class: human

Attributes:
Name
Age
Height

Behaviour
Speak
Work
Sleep

When creating a class, one restricts oneself to the essential features that serve the purpose. These vary depending on the task and the topic.

Let's look at how to create and use a class in Python.

In terms of structure, a class is reminiscent of a mixture of functions and dictionaries. First, the signal word **class** is given, then the name of the class, followed by a colon.

class human:

Unlike functions, the class does not (yet) need any transfer values. Accordingly, the round brackets, as we know them from functions, are omitted.

-ຸ໐ຸ- It is common to start class names with a **capital letter to** distinguish them from variables and functions.

The following lines of code are indented. As with functions and loops, this shows that the code belongs to the framework *class.*

Next, a function is introduced with which an object can be initialised (created). A so-called **constructor is** used for this.

 A constructor is a function for creating a "framework" for an object. It can define the property (attribute) of an object without having to assign a value to it.

For the example, this means that you can use the constructor to set the *name* property, for example, without adding a concrete name. Without this function, one would have to assign a fixed name that applies to every object of the class. If one were to set *name = Tom*, every object created would automatically receive the name *Tom*. Of course, we do not want that. With the help of the constructor, we avoid this situation. Therefore, we use a constructor for each class.

Since the constructor is a function, it is introduced with *def.* This is followed by the expression __*init*__*()*.

 Attention: **Two** underscores must be placed before and after *init*.

Afterwards, values can be passed to the function, which are enclosed in round brackets. A special feature here is that the first transfer value of the constructor must be the expression **self**. The expression is automatically recognised in the Spyder user interface and displayed in red.

 self specifies to the constructor that an object of **its own class** is passed.

Subsequently, further values can be assigned and used within the function (of the constructor).

Within the constructor we define the attributes of the class, in this case the name, the age and the height. For each element of a class, the designation *self.* must be prefixed.

This shows the constructor that the content is assigned to an object variable.

Programming takes some getting used to at first, so we'll go through creating a class using the human class as an example.

In Example, the creation of the class and constructor looks like this:

```
class human:

    def __init__(self,name,age,height,):

        self.name=name #Save the passed variables

        self.age=age

        self.height=height
```

For better clarity, it is advisable to also insert a description of the use of the class as a docstring within a class, just as with the description of a programme.

This description makes it easier for the programmer to understand the background and usefulness of the class.

A reasonable description for the example would be:

```
'''Exercise Classes and Inheritance'''

class human:

    '''Creation of the human Object'''

    def __init__(self,name,age,height,):

        '''The arguments of the human being are defined

        (string) name: name of the person

        (int) age: age of the person

        (float) Height: Height of the human being

        '''

        self.name=name

        self.age=age

        self.height=height
```

This creates a class.

It is useful to list the data types of the attributes and their function.

We now have the basic framework but have not yet created an object. With the help of the classes, however, this is very simple. To do this, we again create an individual name. In our example, we create Tom, who is called the object *human1*.

The object *human1* is created by specifying the class and passing the attributes of the constructor to the class. Internally, the -constructor function is now executed, the attributes are assigned and the object is created.

Each object created has all the attributes of the class.

The spelling is

```
Object = Class(Attribute1,Attribute2,...)
```

Example for our human Class :

```
human1=human("Tom", 26, 1.84)
```

Thus, the first object of the human class has been created. We can read out the individual attributes of the object by naming the object and the desired property.

```
print(human1.name)

print(human1.age)

print(human1.height)
```

> ⇨   Tom
>
> ⇨   26
>
> ⇨   1.84

Individual values of the object can also be entered or overwritten subsequently.

```
human1.name="Tim
```

In the example, the name was changed from *Tom* to *Tim.* From a programming point of view, this is not a problem, but logically it is. Because renaming a person does not make sense (except in individual cases). Since an object represents a real object, we have to address this problem.

Python also offers a method for protecting certain attributes of a class. For this we look at the division of attributes into *public, protected and private.*

5.2.   Encapsulation of classes -public, protected, private

It makes sense to protect individual elements of a class. For example, you should not be able to overwrite a person's name or easily read out a password. Because we can create any kind of attribute; passwords, personal data or internal company content. This opens doors for malicious attackers. For example, if a bank does not protect account data, attackers could easily overwrite account balances.
We have to protect the attributes from the outside world so that access to these elements is no longer possible. The outside world is the main programme or other classes.

This is particularly useful for security reasons, so that sensitive data cannot be read out by a simple command.

> ·ᗜ·   To protect variables from the outside world, you can set them to "**pub-lic**", "**protected**" or "**private**".

But how do we implement this correctly? The previous definition of attributes, where only the variable name is given, shows a public property of the object.

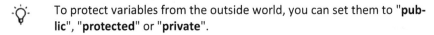

```
self. name=name# this attribute is freely accessible/public
```

The attribute can also be used outside the class.

However, if you put an underscore in front of the variable, it is protected and can only be used within its own class and in subclasses (see next chapter).

A private variable is marked with two underscores and is only available in its own class. Both cases are referred to as encapsulation.

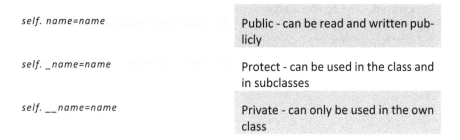

self. name=name	Public - can be read and written publicly
self. _name=name	Protect - can be used in the class and in subclasses
self. __name=name	Private - can only be used in the own class

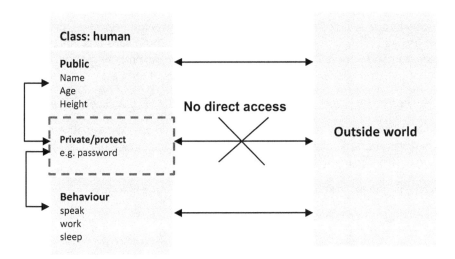

Figure 34Encapsulation of attributes

As the illustration shows, direct access to the attributes is not possible. However, the attributes can still be accessed in a roundabout way, for example via behaviours. This is also intentional. Only direct, uncontrollable access should be prevented. The password can be used within a behaviour. A behaviour in which this is the case would be, for example, "Log into online banking".

However, the encapsulation also creates problems. The name can now no longer be overwritten, but it can also no longer be read out.

The command

```
print(human1.name)        #outputs (actually) the name
```

outputs an error.

In the example, it does not make sense to change the name, but access is also no longer possible, so that it cannot be issued or read out for other purposes. You have gained security, but you have lost functionality. That was not the original idea why we encapsulated variables.

As always, there is a solution in Python.

You can introduce so-called **methods** within a class. With methods, encapsulated attributes can also be processed or output, as we will learn in the following sub-chapter.

5.3. Methods

Methods are very similar to functions in terms of structure. However, methods are defined within a class and are also bound to it. This means that you cannot use a method outside the class, for example in the main programme, with other variables. Methods can only be called with an object of the class.

The constructor __init__() was our first method that we got to know.

Since it is an internal function, the method is created with the signal word *def*. Then we assign an individual name to the function. In our case, the class *human* is to receive the method *Greet*.

Again, arguments can be passed to the method in round brackets.

Here, too, the signal word *self* must be passed as the first value. This shows the interpreter that this is an internal function, a method.

```
def greet(self):

    print('Hello, my name is',self.name)
```

The method outputs the attribute *self. name of* the object.

Although the attribute itself is protected, you can use it within a method and have it output.

The method is called in the main programme like a normal function. Since it is a class-bound function, the object *human1* must also be placed in front.

```
class human:

    '''Creation of the human Object'''

    def __init__(self, name, age, height):

        '''The arguments of the human being are defined

        (string) name: name of the person

        (int) age: age of the person

        (float) Height: Height of the human being

        '''

        self.__name=name #Save the passed variables

        self.__age=age

        self.__height=height

    def greet(self):

        print('Hello, my name is',self. __name)

human1=human("Tom", 26, 1.84)

human1.greet()
```

Methods are also useful for assigning further capabilities to an object of a class. This allows objects to communicate with the user or other objects.

Like functions, methods can be created by the user. In most classes, standard methods are created to change or read protected attributes. It is therefore worth taking a closer look at them.

5.4. Set and Get methods

These methods are often useful for reading or setting attributes in a class. For this purpose, a method is created which changes an attribute **(set)** or outputs the value **(get)**. The name of the method can be chosen freely. However, it is international standard to begin the methods with the words *get* or *set*. A method that outputs the age of the class human should be called *getAge*.

```
    def getAge(self):

        ''' Returns the age '''

                return self.__age # Encapsulated attribute
```

The attribute __age is encapsulated, one can only access the attribute through the method *getAlter*, not through the command *human1.__age*

```
print(human1.getAge()) # Returns the age

print(human1.__age()) ERROR, because encapsulated attribute
```

The aim here is, as already described in the chapter *Encapsulation of Classes, to* allow only **controlled access.**

The *set method* is structured analogously to the *get method*:

```
def setAge(self,new_age):

    ''' Sets the age'''

    self.__age=new_age
```

The method *setAlter* requires the new age as a further transfer variable. The function is again called by the object.

```
human1=human("Tom", 26, 1.84)     #Creates the object human1

print("Age:",human1.getAge())        # Returns the age

human1.setAge("27")                  # Sets the new age

print("New age:", human1.getAge()) # Outputs the new age
```

```
In [21]: runfile('C:/Python_examples/Chapter 5 - OOP/001_Human_Objects.
Age: 26
New age: 27
```

Figure 35Output before and after the setAge command

 Methods can be used to clearly define which rules apply to data within an object. Data can be output, changed or made inaccessible.

Methods can also have a much more complex structure. Just like functions, they are not limited by code.
Another standard method is the del method.

5.5. __del__ method

We already know the *del* function from lists and variables. It can be used to delete not only variables but also objects.

```
del human1
```

The object is removed from the memory. The method is integrated in the inter-preter, similar to a standard function, and was automatically inserted during installation. This means that the method can be applied to **any class** and does not have to be defined in the class.

We can extend the *del* method within a class, for example, to trigger further actions when an object is deleted.

For this purpose, a function with the name __del__ is created within the method.

 When the *del command* is applied to an object of the class, the __del__ method is **automatically** called at the same time.

This can be used, for example, to output a message that the object has been deleted.

The structure of the *del method* is analogous to a normal method. Here, too, the first transfer value is *self.*

```
def __del__(self):
        print("The object was successfully deleted")

del human1
```

```
In [22]: runfile('C:/Python_examples/Chapter 5 - OOP/001_Human_Obj
The object was successfully deleted
```

Figure 36 Output when deleting the object via the del method

This explains the most important properties of classes and methods. Now it's time for the next exercise, in which we will train the encapsulation of variables and the creation of methods.

5.6. Exercise - Password protection

As already mentioned, object-oriented programming is one of the core elements of Python. Therefore, we want to practise dealing with these elements. For this purpose, the *human* class is to be extended by the attribute *Password.* All data such as name, age and height are to be set to **private, so the** attributes cannot simply be read out or changed.

Then create a method that outputs **all** encapsulated attributes after entering (passing) the password. If the password was entered incorrectly, an error message appears.
The distinction whether the password is correct or incorrect is to be realised with an if-query.

5.7. Solution

First, we create the familiar class *human*. Then we create the constructor and pass the attributes of the class to it. In addition, we *add* the new attribute *password*.

```
class human:

    '''Creation of the human Object'''

    def __init__(self, name, age, height, password):

        '''The arguments of the human being are defined

        (string) name: name of the person

        (int) age: age of the person

        (float) Height: Height of the human being

        (string) Password: Password to retrieve data

        '''

        self.__name=name #Save the passed variables

        self.__age=age

        self.__height=height

        self.__password=password
```

Since the class has been extended to include the attribute *password*, one more argument must also be passed. In the example, all attributes are *private*. It is only necessary for the *password attribute.*

The first part of the task has already been completed.
Next, we create the method to match the entered password with the existing password. A suitable name for this is *checkPassword* or also shorter: *checkPW*.

The method for querying the password must be passed a variable *password*.

 Do not confuse: the pass variable *password* is passed from the main programme. The variable *__password* is a private, internal variable of the class.

```
def checkPassword(self,password):

    '''Checks an entered password

        Outputs the data of the class if successful

    '''

    if password==self.__password:
```

```
    print('The password was correct')

    print('The name is:',self.__name)

    print('The age is:',self.__age)

    print('The height is:',self.__height)

else:

    print('The password was not correct')
```

With the help of the if-query, it is checked whether the passed variable matches the internal password. In the positive case, the data is output, otherwise the error message appears.

To test the method, we create an object *human1 of* the class *human*. The attribute *password* is set with *Python3*.

Then we ask the user to enter the password. We store this in the variable *pass_in*.

```
pass_in = str(input("Enter the password \n ",))
```

Then the method *checkPassword* is called. It is passed the password to be checked. We apply the method to the object *human1*.
As a return value we get the data of the object *human1*, or a message that the password was wrong.

```
human1=human("Tom", 26, 1.84, "Python3") #The password is Python3

pass_in = str(input("Enter the password \n "))

human1.checkPassword(pass_in)
```

Let's look at the entire programme code again.

```
''' Exercise Classes Password Protection'''

class human:

    '''Creation of the human Object'''

    def __init__(self, name, age, height, password):

        '''The arguments of the human being are defined

        (string) name: name of the person

        (int) age: age of the person

        (float) Height: Height of the human being

        (string) Password: Password to retrieve data

        '''
```

```python
        self.__name=name
        self.__age=age
        self.__height=height
        self.__password=password
    def checkPassword(self,password):
        '''Checks an entered password
        Outputs the data of the class if successful
        '''
        if password==self.__password:
            print('The password was correct')
            print('The name is:',self.__name)
            print('The age is:',self.__age)
            print('The height is:',self.__height)
        else:
            print('The password was not correct')


human1=human("Tom", 26, 1.84, "Python3") #The password is Python3
pass_in = str(input("Enter the password \n ",))
human1.checkPassword(pass_in)
```

The programme is executed twice. First an incorrect password is entered, then the correct one.

```
In [32]: runfile('C:/Python_examples/Chapter 5 - OOP/002_exercise_passwo

Enter the password
 Python2
The password was not correct

In [33]: runfile('C:/Python_examples/Chapter 5 - OOP/002_exercise_passwo

Enter the password
 Python3
The password was correct
The name is: Tom
The age is: 26
The height is: 1.84
```

Figure 37 check password

5.8. Class variables

All variables or attributes of a class were previously defined in the __init__ method. This means that they apply specifically to each object created. This is also logical, after all, each object has its own individual attributes.

However, there are also properties that affect an **entire class as a unit.** In our example of a human being, this would be the number of persons created. The number of existing people is a variable that is not object-dependent but applies to the whole class.

In Python, a count variable can be created in the main programme that is incremented each time a new object is created.

However, it is also possible to have the counter variables incremented automatically when an object is created. To do this, a global **class variable is** defined within the class. This is placed directly after the class call, before the constructor.

```
class human:

    '''Creation of the human Object'''

    number =0 # global class variable, start value zero

    def __init__(self, name, age, height, password):

        '''The arguments of the human being are defined'''

...
```

The variable *number* is also available for each object created without having to pass it separately.

```
human1=human("Tom", 26, 1.84, "Python3")

print(human1.number)
```

 The query *print(human1.number)* returns the value 0, although the value zero was not explicitly passed when creating the object *human1.*

 The global variable *number* is still the same for each object - namely 0! The variable is not yet changed and therefore does not show the current number of created objects/data sets.

Likewise, the value of the class variable can be accessed directly via the class. For this, **no object** must be created beforehand. To do this, the name of the class is written, followed by a dot and the variable.

```
print(human.number) # Also outputs 0
```

Class variables become interesting when they are combined with methods.

For example, the __init__ and __del__ method can be extended so that the count variable is counted up or down when an object is created or deleted.

human.number =human.number +1

 For the expression *x=x+1* one can also write *x+=1 in* abbreviated form and analogously for *x=x-1* the expression *x-=1*

This shortens the command to

human.number +=1

In addition, further commands can be added, for example

print('A new human being has been born, they now exist', human.number, "humans")

Each time an object is initialised, this message with the new number is also output.

The human class was extended with the methods and the class variable.

```
class human:

    '''Creation of the human Object'''

    number=0 # global class variable, start value zero

    def __init__(self, name, age, height, password):

        '''The arguments of the human being are defined

        (string) name: name of the person

        (int) age: age of the person

        (float) Height: Height of the human being

        '''

        human.number+=1 # Increase class variable by 1

        print('A new human being has been born, they now exist',human.number, "humans")

        self.__name=name #Save the passed variables

        self.__age=age

        self.__height=height

        self.__password=password

    def __del__(self):

        human.number-=1 # Decrease class variable by 1

        print("The object was successfully deleted")

        print('A human has died, they now exist',human.number, "humans")
```

Three objects are created for illustration.

human1=human("Tom", 26, 1.84, "Python3")

human2=human("Lisa", 28, 1.67, "Python3")

human3=human("Kevin", 34, 1.87, "Python3")

del human1

del human2

del human3

At each initialisation, *human.number* is increased by one and the value is output. Subsequently, an object is deleted as an example. In the process, the class variable is decreased by one and also output.

```
In [3]: runfile('C:/Python_examples/Chapter 5 - OOP/003_exercise_counter.py', wd:
A new human being has been born, they now exist 1 humans
A new human being has been born, they now exist 2 humans
A new human being has been born, they now exist 3 humans
The object was successfully deleted
A human has died, they now exist 2 humans
The object was successfully deleted
A human has died, they now exist 1 humans
The object was successfully deleted
A human has died, they now exist 0 humans
```

Figure 37 Output of the variable Man.Number

Class variables are a tool to define a common attribute of all objects. This is exactly what the next programming exercise is about: extending the human class.

5.9. Exercise - Average Height

The average height of all people in a unit is a variable that refers to the whole class of *people*. Nevertheless, the value depends on all existing objects. In this exercise, we extend the class *human* with the class variable *Average height of all objects*.

When a new object is created, the average height is recalculated. For this we need the variable *number,* which was introduced before.

We also need two more class variables, one to store the sums of all body heights and another to represent the average. The following applies:

$$\text{average height} = \frac{\text{total height}}{\text{number of humans}}$$

The calculation can take place in the constructor after an object has been created.

Furthermore, the same calculation must be performed after an object has been deleted.

5.10. Solution

First, the class variables are created and assigned the value zero. The variables were abbreviated in a meaningful way:

```
class human:
    '''Creation of the human Object'''
    number=0 # Global class variable, start value zero
    hgt_tot=0 # Total height of all people
    hgt_avg=0 #Average height of all people
```

Next, we adapt the __init__ method.

Each time a new object is created, the transferred height is summed up and a new average height is calculated.

```
def __init__(self, name, age, height, password):
    '''The arguments of the human being are defined
    (string) name: name of the person
    (int) age: age of the person
    (float) Height: Height of the human being
    '''
    human.number+=1 # Increase class variable by 1
    print('A new human being has been born,now exist', human.number, "humans")
    self.__name=name
    self.__age=age
    self.__height=height
    self.__password=password
    human.hgt_tot+=height          #Recalculate total height
    human.hgt_avg=human.hgt_tot/human.number #Recalculate average
```

To calculate the total height of all objects, we use the passed variable *height*. Alternatively, *self.__height is* also suitable, as the variable was assigned the same value two lines earlier.

The values are summed up and then the value *hgt_avg* is calculated. We see that by calling *human._hgt_avg we* can access the desired value.

Optionally, we can add an output. Here, the average height is again rounded to two decimal places.

```
print('The average height is now', round(human.hgt_avg,2),)
```

Then we perform the same procedure for the __del__ method. This is completed with the same commands. First, the total height is calculated and then the average height.

```
def __del__(self):
    human.number-=1 # Decrease class variable by 1
    print('A human has died, they now exist',human.number, "humans")
    human.hgt_tot-=self.__height #Recalculate total height
    human.hgt_avg=human.hgt_tot/human.number #Recalculate average
    print('The average height is now',round(human.hgt_avg,2),)
```

Finally, a *print() command is* added.

The output is executed by the same calls as in the previous example.

```
human1=human("Tom", 26, 1.84, "Python3")
human2=human("Lisa", 28, 1.67, "Python3")
human3=human("kevin", 34, 1.87, "Python3")
del human1
```

The issue thereby shows:

```
In [1]: runfile('C:/Python_examples/Chapter 5 - OOP/004 exercise Average_Height.
A new human being has been born,now exist 1 humans
The average height is now 1.84
A new human being has been born,now exist 2 humans
The average height is now 1.75
A new human being has been born,now exist 3 humans
The average height is now 1.79
A human has died, they now exist 2 humans
The average height is now 1.77
```

Figure 38 Average height output

Classes, objects, object and class variables are now known. Next, we will look at another major topic of object-optimised programming, the inheritance of classes.

5.11. Inheritance

The division of objects from the real world into classes is clear and easy to understand. When we see a new object, for example a new person, the brain looks for similarities and differences to objects we already know and have memorised. These similarities are compared with empirical values, whereby a classification, better known as "the first impression" of a person, is made within a few seconds.

Our world is a huge, complex system in which many classes influence each other. That is why our brain arranges objects not only into individual classes, but various **subclasses and superclasses.**

As an example, there are different subclasses in the superclass *human. The* classification can be based on geographical origin (*Asians, Europeans, Africans, ...*), age (*babies, children, adolescents, adults, ...*) or other aspects such as profession (*artists, engineers, programmers, ...*). One also speaks of **child classes and parent classes**.

The individual child classes all have the same attributes as the superclass, but can also have additional, individual class attributes.

If one transfers this connection to object-oriented programming, one speaks of **inheritance**.

 The subclasses **inherit** attributes and methods of the parent class. Before creating a subordinate class, the superordinate class must first be created.

The creation of the subclass is identical in structure to the creation of the parent class. However, the name of the superclass must be specified after the class name of the subclass.

As an example, we create a subclass of the class *human*. This contains enthusiastic Python fans, so an appropriate name for the child class is *programmer*.

```
class programmer(human):
```

After the subclass has been created, the constructor of the class is listed again. In this, the arguments of the superclass and optionally others for the subclass are passed. In the example, the subclass *programmer* receives an additional attribute. The attribute *prog_lang* stands for a programming language of the programmer.

```
def __init__(self, name, age, height, prog_lang):
```

 Subsequently, the constructor of the superclass must be called. This creates an object of the superclass within the subclass.

```
human.__init__(self, name, age, height)
```

After the object has been initialised, the attribute *prog_lang* can be defined.

```
self.prog_lang=prog_lang
```

With subclasses, the documentation, i.e. the docstrings, is even more important, as it is easy to overlook that it is a subclass. It is always advisable to clearly mark child classes and the like.

After the subclass has been defined, we can create methods as usual, for example, the *set* and *get methods for the* new value *prog_spr* as well as the *__del__* method. The *set* and *get methods* are not absolutely necessary here because the variable *prog_spr* is not encapsulated. We can simply overwrite or read out its value. Nevertheless, both methods are created as examples.

In the following programme code, the superclass is reduced to the essentials. The password and average height extension from the examples and exercises before are removed again for the sake of clarity. The focus is on the subordinate class.

```
class human:
    ''' Creation of the human Object
    Class variables
    '''

    def __init__(self, name, age, height):
        ''' The arguments of the human being are defined
        (string) name: name of the person
        (int) age: age of the person
        (float) Height: Height of the human '''
        self.__name=name #Save the passed variables
        self.__age=age
        self.__height=height
class programmer(human):
    ''' The class Programmer is a subclass of the class Man
    The class has inherited the following attributes:
```

```
(string) name: name of the person

(int) age: age of the person

(float) Height: Height of the human '''

def __init__(self, name, age, height, prog_lang):

    ''' Class-specific attribute

    (string) prog_lang: Programming language mastered '''

    human.__init__(self, name, age, height)

    self.prog_lang=prog_lang

def getProg_lang(self):

    ''' Outputs current programming language '''

    return self.Prog_lang


def setProg_lang(self,prog_lang_new):

    '''

    Sets new programming language

    '''

    self.Prog_lang=prog_lang_new


def __del__(self):

    print('Unfortunately we have lost a programmer')
```

 In the main programme we can continue to create an object as usual and use the methods of the superclasses and subclasses.

```
programmer1=programmer('Tom',26,1.84,'Python')

print(programmer1.getProg_lang())

del programmer1
```

The programmer *programmer1* is created. It has all the attributes of the super-class and additionally the programming language Python.
Then the method *getProg_lang() is* executed. By executing the method, we get the value of the programming language, in our case *Python*.

Finally, the *del* method is executed and the object is deleted.

5.12. Outsource classes

The previous example shows that classes require an enormous amount of lines. Even though it was a simple subclass where we created a *get and* a *set* method for just one attribute, we ended up with over a pocketbook page of code.

In the Spyder user interface, you can expand and collapse the source code of the classes for this reason.

```
 1  class human:
13
14  class programmer(human):
37
38  programmer1=programmer('Tom',26,1.84,'Python')
39  print(programmer1.getProg_lang())
40  del programmer1
41
```

Figure 39 Folding in and out the programme code in Spyder

This solution works, but the look is still unattractive with multiple classes and many user interfaces do not support this function.

  A more clever variant is therefore, just as with functions, to **outsource** the classes to an **external file.**

The classes human and the subclass Programmer are stored in a separate file *module_classes.py.*

In the main programme there are then many different ways to import the module or the classes of the module. First of all, via the command we already know:

import module_classes

The entire module is imported. In order to access the classes, the path must be specified. This is also familiar to us from procedures such as outsourcing functions to modules.

 # Access via module name.class name

human1= module_classes.human("Tom", 26, 1.84)

programmer1 = module_classes.programmer("Tom", 26, 1.84,'Python')

  Care must be taken to specify the path. If the file *module_classes is* in a sub-folder, this must again be placed in front.

Subfolder.Modulename.Class

This notation is very cumbersome, so there are still alternative variants for importing the classes, which can also be applied to modules with functions.

The command *from module name import class name* can be used to import a single class.

from module_classes import human

The big advantage here is that we don't have to specify the path. We can use the class as if it were in the same programme.

human1= human("Tom", 26, 1.84)

 Several classes and subclasses can also be imported at the same time. The different classes are separated by a comma.

from module_classes import human, programmer

Here, too, we can use the classes without specifying module names

 # Access via module name.class name

human1= module_classes.human("Tom", 26, 1.84)

programmer1 = module_classes.programmer("Tom", 26, 1.84,'Python')

The disadvantage with this variant is that one must specify each class individually. If one wants to use several classes and child classes, all of them must be listed.

A shortcut for specifying all classes is provided by the asterisk operator. Through the command

from module_classes import*

all classes of the module *module_classes* are loaded and can be used without specifying the module.

The disadvantage of using this method is that when importing several modules, one does not know in which module the class used is located. In addition, it is confusing for the understanding of the programme code if an object with a class is suddenly created in a line, which was previously nowhere to be seen concretely. This can be counteracted with detailed documentation. Nevertheless, if only a few classes are needed, it is advisable to import them by naming them specifically.

from module_classes import human, programmer

This command makes it clear that the classes *human* and *programmer* come from the module *module_classes.* In addition, our programming environment Spyder warns us (no error) that we have used the star operator.

The outsourcing of classes is largely identical to that of functions. In the next exercise, we will once again focus on classes and subclasses. A well-known game of chance will be used.

5.13. Exercise - Playing the Lottery

A lottery game is perfect for practising the subject areas such as loops, lists and classes. As an example we use "6 out of 49".

In the 6 out of 49 lottery, 6 numbers are drawn at random from the number series from 1 to 49. Supplements such as additional and super numbers are not taken into account in this example.

For the exercise, the task is divided into the following sub-areas:

1. create a *lottery player* class

The class has the attributes *name* and *Numbers*. The *name of* the player is stored in *name*. In *Numbers,* a list of **six numbers is** stored, which are passed on when a player is created. These correspond to the numbers ticked by the player on the lottery ticket.

Afterwards, create a method *check_win,* which compares the own lottery numbers with the winning numbers and returns the **number of hits**. The easiest way to do this is to create a for-loop that makes an if-query for each winning number.

 The command *x in liste* returns *True if* the element x occurs in the list *liste*, otherwise *False*. This allows us to check whether a winning number matches our own numbers.

Create a total of three different players (objects) with different names and lottery numbers.

Make a list with the numbers 1 to 49.

Pick 6 random numbers out of 49.

 Use the function *random.sample(list1,n) for* this. It returns n random numbers from the list *list1*. For this, the module *random* must be imported via *import random*.

6. compare the winning numbers with the numbers of the lottery players (corresponds to calling the function check_win).

7. have the names and the number of hits for each player.

Since new functions are used and the sequence of commands is somewhat more complex than the previous examples, the following template can serve as a guide. There are, as always in programming, countless other possibilities.

```python
import random

class lottery_player:
    '''
    Creation of the Lottery Player object
    Class variables
    '''

    def __init__(self,name,numbers):
        '''
        The player's arguments are defined
        (string) name: name of the player
        (list) Numbers: List with the player's lottery numbers
        '''

        def check_win(self,win_figures):
            '''
            The player's lottery numbers are
            compared with the winning numbers handed over.
            The number of hits is returned
            '''

### MAIN PROGRAMME###
'''Generating the winning numbers'''
lotto_numbers =range(1,50)
win_figures = random.sample(......)


'''Generating the Players'''


'''Issue of the Winners'''
```

5.14. Solution

First we import the module *random* so that the function *sample()* can be used. The module was automatically downloaded when we downloaded Anaconda. Since it is not part of the built-in libraries, we have to import it.

import random

The *Lottery Player* class is then created. It has no class variables.

Then we assign the attributes name and numbers in the method *__init__*.

import random

class lottery_player:

    '''

    Creation of the Lottery Player object

    Class variables

    '''

    def __init__(self,name,numbers):

        '''

        The player's arguments are defined

        (string) name: name of the player

        (list) Numbers: List with the player's lottery numbers

        '''

        self.name=name

        self.numbers=numbers

Thus, the class has been created, but the method *check_gewinn is* still missing.

The winning numbers are passed to the method in a list with six elements.

Each element of our own list *Numbers* is matched with the winning numbers. A for loop is used for this. If the element is the same, the count variable *hit is* increased by one.

    def check_win(self,win_figures):

        '''

        The player's lottery numbers are

        compared with the winning numbers handed over.

The number of hits is returned

'''

hit=0 # Initially no hit

for x in profit_figures: # For each element in win_numbers

*   if x in self.numbers: # If winning number x exists*

*   hit+=1 # hit +1*

*   return hit # Returns the number of hits*

 There is no *elif* or *else* statement in this if statement. These are not necessary. If the condition is not met, the line *hit+=1 is* skipped and the value *hit is* returned directly.

With the method *check_win* the class is completely defined.

Then we generate the winning numbers with the *range()* and *sample()* functions

lotto_numbers =range(1,50) # Creates a list from 1-49

 # Creates a list with 6 random

win_numbers = random.sample(lotto numbers,6)

After the winning numbers/lotto numbers have been "drawn", three lottery players are created.

These receive six individual lucky numbers, which we can determine ourselves. In the example, six consecutive numbers were chosen for simplification.

'''Generating the Players'''

lottery_player1=lottery_player('Tom',[1,2,3,4,5,6])

lottery_player2=lottery_player('Lisa',[7,8,9,10,11,12])

lottery_player3=lottery_player('Kevin',[13,14,15,16,17,18])

Finally, the command

lottery_player1.name

accessed the name of the player and the number of hits of his numbers by the method call

lottery_player1.check_win(win_numbers)

checked. All this is output in a print command for all players equally.

'''Issue of the Winners'''

```
print("Winning numbers are:",win_numbers)

print(lottery_player1.name, "has",lottery_player1.check_win(win_numbers), "cor-
rect numbers")

print(lottery_player2.name, "has",lottery_player2.check_win(win_numbers), "cor-
rect numbers")

print(lottery_player3.name, "has",lottery_player3.check_win(win_numbers), "cor-
rect numbers")
```

Remark:

In general, it makes more sense to abbreviate variable names, for example *lt_pl1* instead of *lottery_player1*. However, the names of the variables were chosen to be very detailed so that the programme code is easier to understand. Especially at the beginning, this is more important than the compactness of the programme.

This brings us to the end of all the important elements and building blocks of Python programming. Variables, lists, loops, classes, inheritance - we have covered all the topics and programmed small examples.

Everything that follows now is simply importing and applying already existing functions. This is also the focus of Python. We can use existing modules to solve almost any problem.

After we have covered the basics, we will deal with the visual design of the programme, for example by means of graphical user interfaces. To do this, we only need to be able to use the existing functions or methods correctly. There are many different possibilities and libraries available for this. In the following chapter, we will use the most frequently used library, which is also the most suitable for beginners.

6. Create graphic surfaces

Until now, communication with the user of a programme was only realised via the console. The advantages of this are that one can start programming quickly and work in a very code-oriented way. However, the display is not up to date and the input and output options are very limited. If, for example, you forget to enter an inverted comma or write a variable in lower case instead of upper case, such an error can mess up the whole programme. It makes more sense to create windows where the user can select predefined answers by simply clicking a button.

Therefore, in this chapter we deal with a library that can create a graphical user interface.

6.1. Tkinter - various building blocks

A graphical **user interface (GUI)** offers numerous possibilities for displaying or preparing data in a user-friendly way. **Tkinter** is the interface between the Python programming language and the *GUI toolkit TK*, which is used across platforms. A gui toolkit contains modules that have been created by other programmers. With *Tkinter* it is possible to call up windows and design them. In addition, there are numerous other GUI toolkits. However, since *Tkinter* is widely used, we will use it for the upcoming examples. It is included in the Python interpreter by default and therefore does not need to be installed separately.

To import *Tkinter* into the Python programme, the already-known import command is used. Since the Tkinter module contains countless functions, it makes sense to import all functions via the call

from tkinter import* #imports all functions of the module

to import.

 In earlier Python versions, tkinter is written with a capital letter. If you have problems importing, you should update the Python version or try writing *"Tkinter"* instead of *"tkinter"*.

 The Tkinter module is also an **object-oriented module**. It works with classes and objects. Each window we create represents an object of the class Tk. The class Tk is part of the module Tk and does not have to be created separately.

The creation of a window requires an object. The corresponding command is accordingly:

window = Tk()

The class Tk does not require any transfer values.

After the object has been created, various methods can be applied to the object.

 The most essential method from the class *Tk* is the method ***mainloop()***. It opens the object *window*. The command must therefore always be executed last in the main programme, after the settings such as window height, font, etc.

window.mainloop()

After the *window object* has been created, the height can be set. The function required for this is *geometry()*. It is passed a string with the desired pixel width and pixel height.

window.geometry(500x200) # 200 pixels high, 500 pixels wide

Furthermore, a name (title) is assigned to the object.

window.title("Python without prior knowledge")

Tkinter is structured like a kind of construction kit. The *window* object forms the basis. Other objects can be placed on top of this object.

For example, a ***label*** can be applied.

To create a *label object*, the class ***Label*** from the Tkinter library is used.

The object on which the text is set and the text to be displayed are passed to the label. This is done by passing the desired string to the variable *text*.

Similar to the window, the label must then be activated. The ***pack()*** function is used for this.

label = Label(window,text="Python Tkinter Exercise ")

label.pack(expand=1)

This time we set *expand=1* as an argument. This is always necessary if we have adjusted the parent object (window) using the *geometry()* function.

To make the window look like an ordinary Windows window, a **frame is** still missing.

The Frame() method is passed the *window* object and the frame type and width. Then the frame is activated with the *pack()* function. This time the values *fill='both'* and *expand=1* must be called. The variables ensure that both the font and the actual window are framed. The detailed mode of operation is unimportant for the user.

The corresponding commands are

```
frame = Frame(window,relief='ridge',borderwidth=20)

frame.pack(fill='both',expand=1)
```

After the *window*, the caption and the frame have been created, we can run the programme for the first time. The complete programme code is:

```
from tkinter import* #imports all functions of the module

window= Tk()                          #Creates the object

window.geometry('500x200')       # H=200, W=500

window.title("Python without prior knowledge")

label = Label(text='Python Tkinter Exercise')

label.pack(expand=1)

frame = Frame(window,relief='ridge',borderwidth=20)

frame.pack(fill='both',expand=1)

window.mainloop()
```

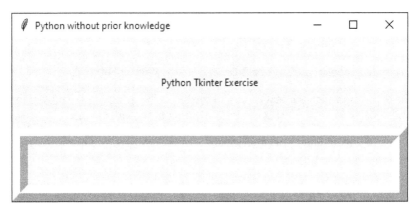

Figure 40 Tkinter window

We have created our first window.

Admittedly, however, this is still very drearily designed. There are no areas, prompts to the user or the like. We now want to change that.

Next, a ***button*** is created with which the window can be closed again. Buttons can be used for a wide range of functions. Their advantage lies in their easy programming and **user-friendly appearance**. When a button is clicked, an **action is** carried out.

For this purpose, the object *window*, the text of the button as well as the height and width are passed to the method *Button()*.

```
button=Button(window,text='EXIT',width=10,height=2)
```

It is important to pass the parent object, in this case the window or frame.

The *button* is then activated using the familiar *pack()* function. We pass the variable *side='bottom'* to the *pack() function.* This places the *button* object at the **bottom**. It is also possible to place it at the top or on the left and right.

```
button.pack(side='bottom')
```

If we execute the programme code, the button is displayed. However, this button has no function yet. We can click it and visual feedback is given, but no function is executed.

The last thing the button needs is a **function or method** that is executed when it is clicked.

A method to close the open window is called *destroy.* To close the *window* object, we write:

```
window.destroy
```

We have to execute this command when we click on the button.

The corresponding attribute that we have to set in the *button* object is called **command**. *Command* is always executed automatically when the button is clicked. If we set *command=window.destroy*, the window will be closed as soon as we click the button.

```
button=Button(window,text='EXIT',width=10,height=2,command=window.destroy)
```

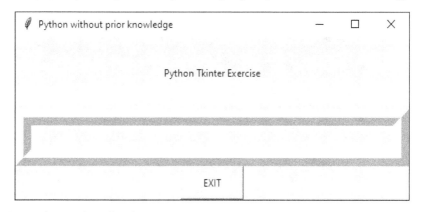

Figure 41 Tkinter window with exit button

We have assigned the *destroy* function to the button. When the button is pressed, the window closes.

 It is also possible to link your **own function to the** button.

As an example, a console output should take place every time the button is pressed.

For this, a corresponding function must first be created.

def output():

  print("The button was pressed")

The function is then assigned to the button.

button=Button(window,text='Click me',width=10,command=output)

 In contrast to a normal function call, we must **omit** the round brackets when assigning. Otherwise, the function is executed directly and not assigned to the attribute *command*.

After we have assigned the function, we call up the window. With each click, the desired output is triggered.

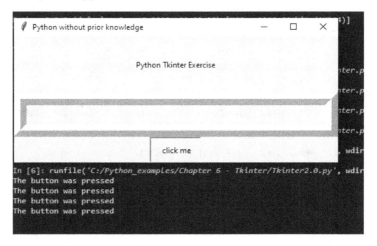

Figure 42Executing your own function via a button

We have assigned the button its own function. Next, the programme is extended. Instead of a *print() command,* the user is to be prompted to enter data.

 To create an input field, the class ***Entry()*** is used. This object must also be unpacked again.

input=Entry() #Creates an input window

input.pack()

The value entered in the input window can be changed by the command

input.get()

can be retrieved. This query is packed into a function, which immediately outputs the value to the console.

```
def read in():
    print(input.get())
```

The function read*()* outputs the read value to the console. Now we simply link the function read*()* with the button press. This works via the familiar assignment

```
command=read
```

This will output the read text to the console when the button is clicked.

 The read text is saved as a string. If you want to read in a number in order to calculate with it later, the data type must be changed to int() or float().

```
x= input.get()      #Read number is saved as a string
```

```
x= int(input.get()) #Input number is saved as an Int number
```

We also change the text of the button from *EXIT* to *Read.* The entire code results in:

```
from tkinter import* #imports all functions of the module
def output():
    print("The button was pressed")
def read(): # Outputs the read value
    print(input.get())
window= Tk()                      #Creates the object
window.geometry('500x200')        # H=200, W=500
window.title("Python without prior knowledge")
label = Label(window,text='Python Tkinter Exercise')
label.pack(expand=1)
frame = Frame(window,relief='ridge',borderwidth=20)
frame.pack(fill='both',expand=1)
button=Button(window,text='Read',width=10,height=2,command=read)
button.pack(side='bottom')
input=Entry() #Creates an input window
input.pack()
window.mainloop()
```

We start the programme, the window opens. You can see the button and an input window. We enter a sample text. When we click the button, the text is output to the console.

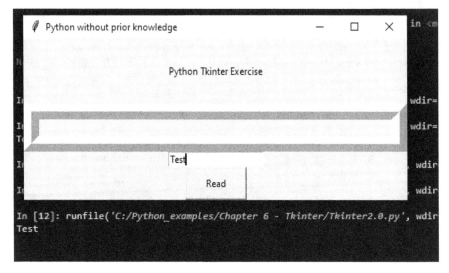

Figure 43 Input window with console output

 The class Entry contains an attribute ***insert***. If we pass it a string, it appears in the entry box. For this, a **zero** must be passed as the first element, and the desired text or number as the second element.

input.insert(0,'default value') #inserts the value into the field

This is helpful, for example, to set a **default value in** the input field.

In addition, we can use the input box as an **output element** at the same time.

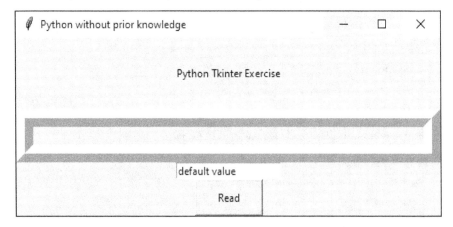

Figure 44 Input box with default value

In addition, one can check the entered or output values with the function

input.delete(0,'end')

delete. This is useful if you perform several actions and otherwise the input/output box overflows.

Input/output windows are essential tools for communicating with the user via a window. In addition, the console can always be included.

Next, we will add a **scroll bar.** This is a field with predefined choices. By scrolling in the field, you can select the appropriate element.

For this purpose, the command

Scrollbar = Scrollbar(window)

is called. The function **Scrollbar(),** which is also an element of the *Tkinter* module, receives the object *window* as a transfer value. Within the field, a box with a list of elements is to be displayed. To do this, we use the **Listbox()** function, which requires an input variable **yscrollcommand**. We must assign our variable *scrollbar to* this, whereby a *set command* must also be appended.

listbox=Listbox(window,yscrollcommand=scrollbar.set)

Our *listbox* has been created. We now only have to fill it with values. The easiest way to do this is to use the *insert command*. The elements are to be placed at the end, so we pass the value **END.**

We create a list with any elements. Then we append the individual elements of the *list* to our list *box with the* help of a *for loop.*

listbox=Listbox(window,yscrollcommand=scrollbar.set)

list1=range(100)   #list for list box 0..100

for element in list1:   # As long as elements in the list

   listbox.insert(END,element)   #Append list element

Next, we have to **configure** the *scrollbar*. This means that we make sure that the box also changes at the same time as we scroll with the mouse. The already known *command attribute is* set here to **listbox.yview**

scrollbar.config(command=listbox.yview)

Finally, we display both objects. So that the scrollbar and the listbox are on top of each other, we set *side='left' for* **both objects**.

listbox.pack(side="left")

scrollbar.pack(side = "left", fill = 'both')

The entire code looks like this:

```
from tkinter import* #imports all functions of the module
window= Tk()                        #Creates the object
window.geometry('500x200')         # H=200, W=500
window.title("Python without prior knowledge")
scrollbar=Scrollbar(window)
listbox=Listbox(window,yscrollcommand=scrollbar.set)
list1=[1,2,3,4,5,6,7,8,9,10] #list for listbox
for element in list1: # As long as there are elements in the list
    listbox.insert(END,element) #Append list element
scrollbar.config(command=listbox.yview)
listbox.pack(side="left")
scrollbar.pack(side = "left", fill = 'both')
window.mainloop()
```

After running the programme, we get the desired *scroll box* with our list as elements to select.

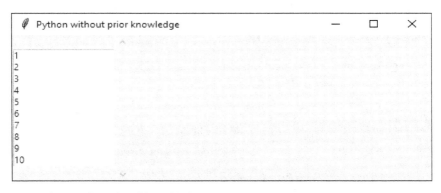

Figure 45Tkinter window with scroll bar and list box

If we want to trace the selected element, we can find the index of the element or the row in which the number stands via the function

```
listbox. curselection()
```

Next, we look at the programming of **checkboxes** or **checkbuttons.** A checkbox is a field that the user can either click on (check) or leave open during a query. Since the checkbox can only have two states (checked or not), the result will be a variable of type *bool,* i.e. 1 for *True* or 0 for *False*. This variable must first be created. The *IntVar()* function is used for this.

```
check=IntVar()
```

Strictly speaking, this is not a function, but a separate class that creates an object. Then the actual checkbox is created. This requires the window, the variable *check* and a function as transfer values. The function is always executed as soon as the checkbox is clicked or the selection is deleted again.

```
check=IntVar()

checkbutton=Checkbutton(window,text="Python3",variable=check,command = read)
```

In our example, we use a separate function *read()*, which outputs to the console whether the checkbox was clicked or not. With the help of the *get command*, the state of the checkbox (*True or False*) can be determined.

```
def einlesen(): # Outputs the read value

  if check.get():

    print('Checkbox is selected')

  else:

    print('Checkbox is not selected')
```

Finally, the checkbox is reactivated with the *pack()* function.

```
checkbutton.pack()
```

In summary, this results in the programme code:

```
from tkinter import* #imports all functions of the module

window= Tk()                      #Creates the object

window.geometry('500x200')        # H=200, W=500

window.title("Python without prior knowledge")

def einlesen(): # Outputs whether checked or not

  if check.get():

    print('Checkbox is selected')

  else:

    print('Checkbox is not selected')

check=IntVar() #Check variable

checkbutton=Checkbutton(window,text="Python3",variable=check,command = read)

checkbutton.pack()

window.mainloop()
```

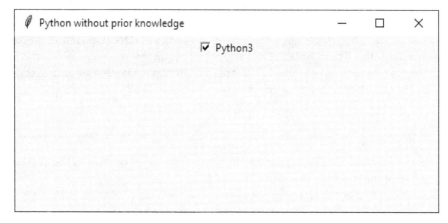

Figure 46Tkinter window with checkbox

The checkbox is selected and deselected. In the meantime, the console outputs the following:

```
In [17]: runfile('C:/Python_examples/Chapter 6 - Tk
Checkbox is selected
Checkbox is not selected
Checkbox is selected
```

Figure 47Console output when the checkbox is selected and deselected

Each time a selection or deselection is made, the read() function is executed and a console output is triggered.

With the checkbox we have got to know the last element of the Tkinter family.

After we have covered the most important building blocks of graphic programming, we move on to the visual design. Before that, the concluding table shows all the important classes and their function.

Class	Function	Example
Tk()	Windows	*window= Tk()*
Label	Text field	*label = Label(window,text='Python Tkinter Exercise')* *label.pack(expand=1)*
Frame	Frame	*frame = Frame(window,relief='ridge',borderwidth=20)*
Button	Button/Field	*button=Button(window,text='Read')*
Entry	Input field	*input=Entry() #Creates an input window*
Scrollbar Listbox	Scrollbar with a list	*Scrollbar = Scrollbar(window)* *listbox=Listbox(window,yscrollcommand=scrollbar.set)*
Checkbox	Checkbutton	*check=IntVar() #Check variable* *checkbutton=Checkbutton(window,* *text="Python3",* *variable=check,command = read in)*

6.2. Visual design of the windows

Our intention for programming windows was to create a more user-friendly environment. With the methods we have learned, we have only succeeded to a limited extent so far. The buttons and windows already fulfil their purpose, but the layout still leaves a lot to be desired. Therefore, in this subchapter we look at some possibilities to optimise the layout of the window, to display pictures and to colour texts.

6.3. The grid manager

Python, or *tkinter*, has a **layout manager** integrated for this purpose. Under the name *grid,* a **grid-like structure** can be placed over the window, which divides the window into different segments. To do this, we first need to know how many **rows** and **columns** our window should be divided into. If we want to place the object *button in* the first row and first column, we write the instruction:

```
button.grid(row=0,column=0) # Index starts at zero
```

With the help of the *grid manager* we can determine the arrangement of the elements, i.e. the buttons as well as the input or text fields.

For the visual representation of the grid system, we create **four buttons** (*button1 - button4)* and arrange them with the help of the *grid command*.

```
from tkinter import* #imports all functions of the module

window= Tk()                        #Creates the object

button1=Button(window,text='Button1',width=10)

button1.grid(row=0,column=0)

button2=Button(window,text='Button2',width=10)

button2.grid(row=0,column=1)

button3=Button(window,text='Button3',width=10)

button3.grid(row=1,column=0)

button4=Button(window,text='Button4',width=10)

button4.grid(row=1,column=1)

window.mainloop()
```

The buttons are laid out in a total of two rows and two columns.

If we use the grid manager, it places the objects in the desired positions. This means we no longer need the *pack()* function.

 We must never use the *grid()* and *pack()* functions in the same window. Otherwise an error will be displayed.

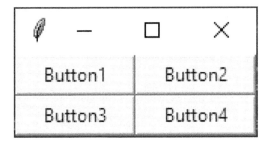

Figure 48 Tkinter representation using the grid manager

In addition to the column and row specifications, it is also possible to specify over how many columns and rows the element is to be placed. The commands for this are:

columnspan = 2, rowspan = 2 # Element placed over two rows and columns

In addition, distances between two elements can be added. With the attributes **padx** and **pady** we can specify distances in X-direction and Y-direction.

As an example, we expand our four buttons. We insert an X-distance of 10 and a Y-distance of 10 between the buttons. In order to find out the appropriate distances, we have to try something until it is visually appealing.

In addition, buttons 3 and 4 are combined into one button that extends over **two** fields. To do this, button 3 is placed in the middle of two fields.

button3.grid(row=1,column=0,columnspan=2,padx=10,pady=10)

The code is thus extended as follows:

```
from tkinter import* #imports all functions of the module

window= Tk()                    #Creates the object

button1=Button(window,text='Button1',width=10)

button1.grid(row=0,column=0,padx=10,pady=10)

button2=Button(window,text='Button2',width=10)

button2.grid(row=0,column=1,padx=10,pady=10)

button3=Button(window,text='Button3',width=10)

button3.grid(row=1,column=0,columnspan=2,padx=10,pady=10)

window.mainloop()
```

A new window opens.

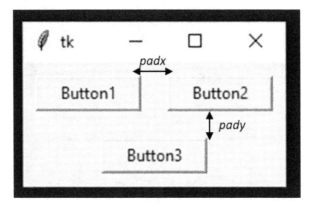

Figure 49 Extension of the grid manager

That already looks much better than before.

 By structuring the elements, we can build a window in a much more user-friendly way.

6.4. Place Manager

We have discussed the placement of elements with the help of a grid. An even more flexible option is to place objects with the help of the **place manager**. Here you specify the concrete x and y coordinates to which the object is to be aligned. The zero point is the upper left corner of the window.

We take the previous example and realise it with the help of the Place Manager:

```
from tkinter import* #imports all functions of the module

window= Tk()                    #Creates the object

window.geometry('300x100')       # H=200, W=500

button1=Button(window,text='Button1',width=10)

button1.place(x=50, y=20)

button2=Button(window,text='Button2',width=10)

button2.place(x=150, y=20)

button3=Button(window,text='Button3',width=10)

button3.place(x=100, y=70)

window.mainloop()
```

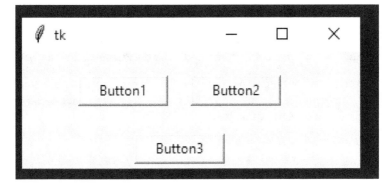

Figure 50Placement of the buttons by the place manager

 Finding the right coordinates is possible by trying several times. There-fore, the division into rows and columns is preferred whenever possible.

Nevertheless, the Place Manager has its advantages, for example, if a sketch of the user interface with measurements (e.g. in cm) is already available. In that case we can convert the distances directly into pixels.

In general, it should be mentioned that aligning to concrete coordinates is not only limited to buttons. Input fields, text fields and even pictures can also be placed in this way. We will look next at how we can include images in the window.

6.5. Loading PNG files

A picture says more than 1000 words. Therefore, the presentation of pictures must not be missing in user-oriented programming.

If we want to display an image, it must first be saved as a PNG file. Jpg files are also possible as an alternative. Other data formats are only supported in a round-about way. The path of the file must be known. For the example, the image py-thon.png is stored in the path

C:\Python_Exercises\python.png

To load the picture, a variable *img is* created. The photo is passed to it. This is possible with the function **PhotoImage().** We have to set *file=r* (read) and specify the path of the image to be loaded.

img = PhotoImage(file = r "C:\Python_Exercises\python.png")

To adjust the height of the image, the command

img1 = img.subsample(2,2)

is used.

 This reduces the resolution and thus the height of the image. If we use a different image, this command must be adapted accordingly.

Trial and error usually helps. The command is not necessary for the example. The image is stored in the variable *img1*. To display it on the window, we use the *Label()* class. We pass the variable to it.

```
label_img=Label(window, image = img)
```

```
Label_img.grid()
```

We then combine the individual code parts into one overall code.

```
from tkinter import *
window = Tk()
window.title("Python without prior knowledge")
img = PhotoImage(file = r"C:\Python_examples\Chapter 6 - Tkinter\python.png")
label=Label(window, image = img)
label.grid()
mainloop()
```

Figure 51 Displaying an image via PhotoImage()

With the importing of images, some colour has literally come into the display for the first time. This is exactly where we want to continue by highlighting objects such as text fields in colour.

6.6. Highlight objects in colour

So far, we have adjusted the arrangement and display. The fields remained grey until now, only the imported images were displayed in colour.

Classes such as the *Label()* class already have attributes for specifying the colour of the object. That is, without further specification, the familiar shade of grey is used by default. However, you can define the colour of the background as well as the colour of the font, the height and even the font itself.

We have to set the following attributes for this:

Fg -font colour : red,green,yellow,pink,...

bg - Background colour: red,green,yellow,pink,...

font - Font and style: Normal,Bold,Italic,Roman... Height: 12,16,24...

The attributes for *fg* and *bg* are passed as a string. *Font* requires the font as a string and the height as a number.

window,text='Large',fg='white',bg='red',font=('Arial',48)

As an example, three different text fields are created, each with a different background colour, font colour, font height and font style.

```
from tkinter import*

window= Tk()                          #Creates the object

window.title("Python without prior knowledge")

#Creating the label

label1 = Label(window,text='Large',fg='white',bg='red',font=('Arial',48))

label2 = Label(window,text='medium',fg='pink',bg='green',font=('Roman',32))

label3 = Label(window,text='Small',fg='black',bg='yellow',font=('Bold',16))

#Categorising the labels

label1.grid(row=0,column=0,pady=10)

label2.grid(row=1,column=0,pady=10)

label3.grid(row=2,column=0, pady=10)

window.mainloop()
```

The top field has a red background with white lettering. The font is Arial and the font height is 48 points.

The second box has a green background with pink lettering. The font style is Roman and the font height is 32 points.

The last field has a yellow background with black lettering. The font style is Bold and the font height is 16 points.

Figure 52 Displaying different font heights, colours and fonts

The appropriate attributes, such as the colours and fonts that can be used, can be found on the official *tkinter page:*

https://docs.python.org/3/library/tk.html

For existing objects, the attributes can also be read out or overwritten.

The method *cget* is used to read out an attribute. Overwriting a value is done with the method *config.*

print(label1.cget('font')) #Font values are read and output

label1.config(font=('Roman',32)) #Font is overwritten

print(label1.cget('font')) #Font values are read and output

```
In [4]: runfile('C:/Python_examples/Chapter 6 - Tkint
Tkinter')
Arial 48
Roman 32
```

Figure 53Reading out the text parameters

With this, we have gone through the most important building blocks for the presentation of a GUI. In the following exercise, we will apply what we have learned to create a visually appealing GUI.

6.7. Exercise-Calculator

In the following, the graphical representation is to be practised on the basis of the creation of a pocket calculator. The task for this is as follows:

1. create a heading "Calculator"

2. create two input fields, each with a number entered.

Create four check boxes with the names *plus, minus, times and divided*. The choice of checkbox determines the operator to be used.

Create an input/output field for the result.

Create a button that calculates the result and inserts it into the input field.

6. Optional: Set font heights, background colours and other attributes for all elements. In addition, incorrect entries can be intercepted if more than one or no checkbox is selected.

The result could look like this:

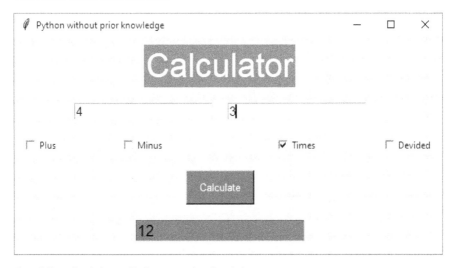

Figure 54Example solution graphical representation of a calculator

6.8. Solution

First, we create the basic framework. The libraries are imported.

```
window= Tk()                        #Creates the object
window.geometry('570x280')          # H=280, W=570
window.title("Python without previous knowledge")
```

Next, we define the heading *label1,* our four *check buttons 1-4,* the two input fields *input1 and input2,* our confirmation button *button1* and the output field *output1.* Before we can create the check buttons, we have to create four variables *check1-4,* which store the content of the respective box.

```
check1=IntVar() #Check variable Plus

check2=IntVar() #Check variable minus

check3=IntVar() #Check variable Mal

check4=IntVar() #Check variable Divided
```

After that we can create all the elements. The individual elements were simultaneously assigned different heights, background colours and font colours.

```
label1 = Label(window,text='calculator',fg='white',bg='grey',font=('Arial',32))

button1=Button(window,text='Calculate',width=10,height=2,command=output,
          fg='white',bg='green',font=('Arial',10))

input1=Entry(fg='black',bg='yellow',font=('Arial',12))

input2=Entry(fg='black',bg='yellow',font=('Arial',12))

output1=Entry(fg='black',bg='green',font=('Arial',15))
```

And the checkboxes:

```
checkbutton1=Checkbutton(window,text="Plus",variable=check1)

checkbutton2=Checkbutton(window,text="Minus",variable=check2)

checkbutton3=Checkbutton(window,text="Mal",variable=check3)

checkbutton4=Checkbutton(window,text="Shared",variable=check4)
```

We do not need to pass a function for the checkboxes, as nothing should happen when a box is selected or deselected. Only when clicking on *button1* should the function *output()* be executed.

The function *output*() first checks whether more than one box has been activated. To do this, it checks whether the sum of all *check variables* is greater than 1. If this is the case, the output variable *output is* set to *'Several selected'.*

```
def output():
  if (check1.get()+check2.get()+check3.get()+check4.get() >1):
    output='several selected'
```

If only one checkbox is active, the values in the input fields are read in.

Since they are stored as strings, a type conversion to integer must still take place.

```
  else:
    number1=int(input1.get())
    number2=int(input2.get())
```

The individual cases are then processed and each *check variable is* checked. Accordingly, the previously read-in data is calculated and saved in the output variable.

```
  if check1.get():
      output = number1+number2
  elif check2.get():
      output = number1-number2
  elif check3.get():
      output = number1*number2
  elif check4.get():
      output = round(number1/number2,2)
  else:
      output='Select: +,-,*,/'
```

When dividing, the numbers are additionally rounded, as infinite-period fractions can occur.

If none of the four boxes is selected, the output variable is overwritten with *'Select from: +,-,*,/'*.

In any case, the output field is cleared and then the result (or error) is output.

```
  output1.delete(0,'end')
  output1.insert(0,output)
```

The last step is to place all objects. The *grid manager* was used for this. The *place manager* works in the same way. The entire programme code develops as follows:

```python
from tkinter import* #imports all functions of the module
def output():
  if (check1.get()+check2.get()+check3.get()+check4.get() >1): #optinal if
    output='several selected'
  else:
    number1=int(input1.get())                #Adapt data type of string
    number2=int(input2.get())
    if check1.get():
      output = number1+number2
    elif check2.get():
      output = number1-number2
    elif check3.get():
      output = number1*number2
    elif check4.get():
      output = round(number1/number2,2)
    else:
      output='Select: +,-,*,/'
  output1.delete(0,'end')     # Note indentation, will always be executed
  output1.insert(0,output)


window= Tk()                  #Creates the object
window.geometry('570x280')    # H=280, W=570
window.title("Python without prior knowledge")
label1 = Label(window,text='calculator',fg='white',bg='grey',font=('Arial',32))
button1=Button(window,text='Calculate',width=10,height=2,command=output,
       fg='white',bg='green',font=('Arial',10))
input1=Entry(fg='black',bg='yellow',font=('Arial',12))
input2=Entry(fg='black',bg='yellow',font=('Arial',12))
output1=Entry(fg='black',bg='green',font=('Arial',15))
'''CHECKFIELDS'''
check1=IntVar() #Check variable Plus
check2=IntVar() #Check variable minus
```

```
check3=IntVar() #Check variable Mal
check4=IntVar() #Check variable Divided
checkbutton1=Checkbutton(window,text="Plus",variable=check1)
checkbutton2=Checkbutton(window,text="Minus",variable=check2)
checkbutton3=Checkbutton(window,text="Times",variable=check3)
checkbutton4=Checkbutton(window,text="Devided",variable=check4)
'''GRID-MANAGER'''
label1.grid(row=0,column=1,padx=10,pady=10,columnspan=2)
input1.grid(row=1,column=1,padx=10,pady=10)
input2.grid(row=1,column=2,padx=10,pady=10)
checkbutton1.grid(row=2,column=0,padx=10,pady=10)
checkbutton2.grid(row=2,column=1,padx=10,pady=10)
checkbutton3.grid(row=2,column=2,padx=10,pady=10)
checkbutton4.grid(row=2,column=3,padx=10,pady=10)
button1.grid(row=3,column=1,columnspan=2,pady=10)
output1.grid(row=4,column=1,columnspan=2,pady=10)
window.mainloop()
```

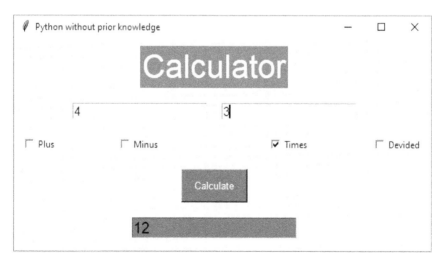

Figure 55Reactions of the calculator with different choices

That was not only the end of the exercise, but also of this book - almost! Because a chapter that is becoming more and more important should not remain unmentioned. It shows the possibilities that can easily be implemented with Python. We are talking about **artificial intelligence** and **neural networks**. Most companies already use Python as an industry standard for neural networks and machine learning.

7. Artificial intelligence and neural networks

One of the topics that has been on everyone's lips for years is **artificial intelligence, or AI** for **short.** In connection with the buzzword AI, terms such as **neural networks, machine learning or deep learning are** often thrown into the room.

It therefore makes sense to first explain the different terms.

 Artificial intelligence (AI) is the **umbrella term** under which all other terms are subsumed. AI refers to the imitation or simulation of human intelligence by means of machines, nowadays almost exclusively computers or entire computer systems.

Special sequences of functions are used for this purpose. These function structures are called **algorithms.**

 Artificial intelligence uses computer algorithms that adapt and improve themselves.

The term neural networks, on the other hand, refers to a way in which the learning algorithms are constructed. Machine learning, deep learning etc. describes the process of improving a neural network, i.e. the constant adaptation of the network: the network "learns".

Before we get to the construction of a neural network, let's first look at what the advantages are of using artificial intelligence.

The aim of the following chapters is not to have understood the construct of artificial intelligence down to the smallest detail. That would be more than beyond the scope of this book. Instead, the basic principles are explained and examples in Python are covered, so that if you are interested, you can delve into the subject area in more detail.

7.1. Aim and benefit of an AI

Before we programme an AI, we first clarify the question of what AIs are useful for in the first place.

 AIs analyse huge amounts of data and find correlations between factors that influence an outcome. They can use past data to make **forecasts for the future.**

Let's take the stock market as an example. Shares in companies are very volatile, which means that the price rises and falls constantly. Even experts who spend their whole lives studying the mechanisms behind share prices have not managed to reliably predict a company's share price. This is because many factors play a role in the price of a share: the profits of the companies, the expectations of the people who buy the share and even political and geographical disputes of states.

Nobody knows the exact factors 100%; theoretically, it could also be that a share rises rather than falls in good weather. This sounds absurd, but there are numerous factors that could potentially influence the price of a share.

A simple human being cannot oversee this amount of influences. And this is exactly where an AI could come into play.

An AI can use existing data to recognise correlations and calculate future events. For example, an AI analyses the behaviour of all buyers and sellers, political correlations and much more. In the end, it makes a prediction about the development of the share. The more data the AI has and the longer it has been trained, the more accurate the forecast. At the moment, no AI has yet succeeded in reliably predicting share prices.

 If we fed an AI all the data that has ever existed and trained it infinitely, the AI would be able to predict everything that would ever happen. It would be omniscient. It could predict share prices, when and where a person would be born or how long we would all live.

Admittedly, this is an absurd example that will probably never become real. A computer could never process so much data and training would take an infinitely long time. But this example shows us where the journey is heading. More and more information, more and more computing power. It is not for nothing that Google, Amazon and others are collecting more and more user data and expanding their data centres.

Figure 56 Corridor of a server room with hundreds of computers

The idea of an all-knowing artificial intelligence seems a little scary at first, but we should not only see the negative. AI is an opportunity. We could achieve breakthroughs in science, autonomous driving is on the horizon and maybe the next super-computer will find a cure for cancer. In any case, artificial intelligence is an area where there is a lot of potential. It is worthwhile getting to grips with it. So we now know what an AI is capable of and what advantages it offers. Let's now take a look at how an AI or a neural network is built.

7.2. Structure of a neural network

The model for the construction of neural networks is provided by the most powerful computer of all - our brain! The human brain is significantly more efficient than any computer ever developed. It consists of individual **neurons** that are complexly interconnected by **synapses.**

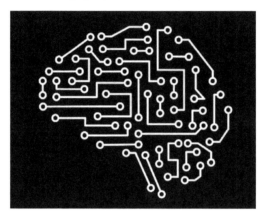

Figure 57Networked brain

An artificial neural network is constructed according to this model. Different neurons are created, which learn how they must be linked to each other in order to find the optimal result for a defined task. The creation of these connections requires **data, time and computing power**.

A neuron is also called a **tensor**. The neurons are structured in different layers.

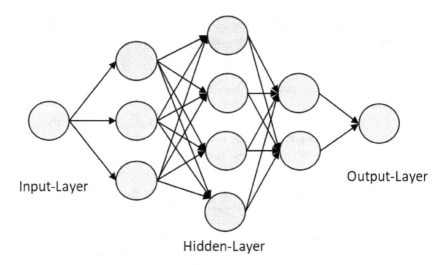

Input-Layer

Output-Layer

Hidden-Layer

Figure 58 3 Layered structure of a neural network

A neural network normally has at least three layers. In the first layer, the data is input (**input layer**). In the second (third, etc) layer, the data is processed and combined (**hidden layer**) and finally output in the last (**output layer**). As can be seen in the drawing, all neurons have connections to the others. The connections between the neurons are called **synapses in reference to** the human brain.

There are many other ways to set up a neural network. One of them is that not only do the previous neurons have an influence on the next layer, but that the individual neurons can influence themselves. For the general understanding, the concrete design and construction of the different structures are irrelevant. The principles can be applied to all structures.

7.3. How does a neural network learn?

A neural network has the advantage that it becomes more and more accurate as time goes on. The more data it is fed, the more effective and the more efficient the network becomes.

The term "train" mentioned earlier refers to running through cycles and improving the connections of the neurons. The runs are also called cycles.

But what does this training look like in concrete terms? To do this, we first need to understand that an AI does not initially have any internal content and data. Let's take two data series as an example.

input=[1,2,3,4,5]

output=[3,6,9,12,15]

The connection between the two series should be clear to everyone right away. Each element of the second row is three times the matching element of the first row. However, an AI does not know this at the beginning.

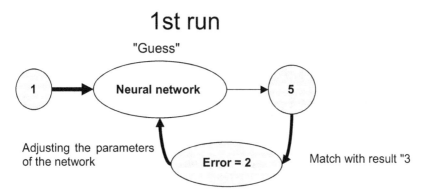

1st run

"Guess"

Adjusting the parameters of the network

Match with result "3

Figure 59 First training run of an AI

The AI first tries to find random correlations between the data sets. To do this, it takes an element from the input data series and predicts an output value for this value. Then the AI compares the calculated result with the correct result from the output list and adjusts its links so that the result is closer to the desired result in the next run. This is tried for all data from the data sets so that in the end all calculated data are as close as possible to the output data set.

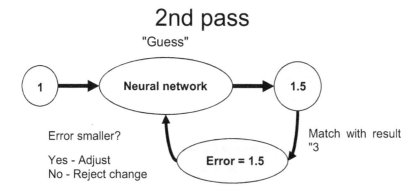

2nd pass

"Guess"

Error smaller?

Yes - Adjust
No - Reject change

Match with result "3

Figure 60 Second training run of an AI

At first, nonsensical, random connections are formed, which are later dissolved again. Little by little, links are formed that come closer and closer to the desired result. With each new run, the result becomes more accurate and comes closer to the correct values.

As a result, internal circuits are formed that become more and more accurate.

 In a real neural network, each number is not run through individually, as in the illustration, but always all numbers simultaneously, in order to include cross-dependencies. In our example, this would be to check whether the other data in the data series, for example the numbers *[2,3,4,5],* also have an influence on the result *2.*

If, after the network has been trained, we feed in new, previously unknown data, for example the number 10, the network must calculate the appropriate answer to this number itself.

The network will determine an approximation of the result through the already known data, in our case this would optimally be the number 30. In practice, the result will deviate somewhat from this, whereby the deviation becomes smaller and smaller with the number of runs.

In principle, this already explains the structure of an artificial intelligence. A neural network consisting of several layers and many neurons is created. Data must then be fed into the network. Through training, the network improves the internal connections and brings the result for future values closer and closer to the true value.

Of course, the example shows the simplest form of a neural network with only one input and one output list. In reality, the data is complex, so that one usually no longer has a complete overview of it. The internal states of the neurons and their origins are also no longer comprehensible in most cases.

Next, we look at its realisation in Python. For this we use existing modules.

7.4. Data stream optimised programming

Python is gaining more and more popularity. One aspect is object-oriented programming OOP. Another aspect is the easy programming of neural networks.

 Since neural networks process data internally and the data is changed step by step in the different layers and then passed on to the next layer, this is also referred to as **data stream optimised programming**.

By simply using existing libraries, we can create a neural network within a very short time. The library needed for this is the ***tensorflow*** library.

The *tensorflow* library was designed by Google. Compared to a private library, Google as a large corporation has virtually unlimited financial resources. The library was created by professional developers. *Tensorflow* is very reliable and is regularly updated. The **open-source deep learning library *Keras*,** a sub-library based on tensorflow, contains the functions we need to build a neural network.

Keras can also be imported independently of *tensorflow*. *Keras* is a private library.

The libraries are not installed in the Python interpreter. Therefore, we must first install the desired library and enter the following command directly into the console.

pip install keras

pip install tensorflow

If the command does not work, you can alternatively use the command

conda install -c conda keras

conda install -c conda tensorflow

can be used. More detailed installation instructions can be found at https://github.com/keras-team/keras.

Windows users may need to start the programme "*Anaconda Prompt*". To do this, we must search for *Anaconda Prompt in* the Start directory or in the Windows search bar.

The entry is then confirmed with Enter. If necessary, we have to restart the Spyder programme before and after this.

The libraries *keras* and *tensorflow* and others are automatically installed.

```
 ▢   Console 1/A

In [1]: conda install -c conda keras
Collecting package metadata (current_repodata.json): ...working... done
Solving environment: ...working... failed with initial frozen solve. Retrying with flexible solve.
Solving environment: ...working... failed with repodata from current_repodata.json, will retry with next repodata source.
Collecting package metadata (repodata.json): ...working... done
Solving environment: ...working... done

## Package Plan ##

  environment location: C:\Users\user\anaconda3

  added / updated specs:
    - keras


The following packages will be downloaded:

    package                    |            build
    ---------------------------|-----------------
    _tflow_select-2.2.0        |            eigen          3 KB
    absl-py-0.11.0             |    py37haa95532_0        169 KB
    astor-0.8.1                |           py37_0         47 KB
    gast-0.4.0                 |            py_0          15 KB
    grpcio-1.27.2              |   py37h351948d_0        1.2 MB
    importlib-metadata-2.0.0   |            py_1          35 KB
    keras-2.3.1                |             0            6 KB
    keras-applications-1.0.8   |            py_1          29 KB
    keras-base-2.3.1           |           py37_0        485 KB
    keras-preprocessing-1.1.0  |            py_1          37 KB
    libprotobuf-3.13.0.1       |       h200bbdf_0        1.8 MB
    markdown-3.3.3             |    py37haa95532_0        167 KB
    protobuf-3.13.0.1          |    py37ha925a31_1        535 KB
    tensorboard-1.14.0         |    py37he3c9ec2_0        3.1 MB
    tensorflow-1.14.0          | eigen_py37hcf3f253_0        5 KB
    tensorflow-base-1.14.0     | eigen_py37hdbc3f0e_0     34.3 MB
    tensorflow-estimator-1.14.0|            py_0         261 KB
    termcolor-1.1.0            |           py37_1          8 KB
    ---------------------------|-----------------
                                         Total:        42.2 MB
```

Figure 61Installing the required libraries

After installing the libraries, we can import them as usual. So that we do not have to specify the full module name *tensorflow* or *keras each* time, we import all functions

from tensorflow import*

from keras import*

Next, we create a neural network.

The function *models.Sequential()* from the Keras library is used for this. We could name the neural network *net1* or *neur_net,* for example.

In Keras, it has become accepted to call a neural network a **model**. Since many help pages and example texts use the same designation, we will stick to this term.

model = models.Sequential()

With this, we have created our first neural network. This does not yet contain any layers or neurons. The network is the **basic framework** into which we can insert layers and neurons. Before we create the layers and neurons, we first need to know how many input neurons we need. We remember that the input layer is the very first layer that receives the input data.

To determine the input height, we use our two data sets.

Input_list=[1,2,3,4,5]

Output_list=[3,6,9,12,15]

 The data sets consist of 5 elements. However, the number of neurons does not depend on the number, but on the dimension of the data! In our case, the input of the first layer and the output of the last layer may only contain one neuron!

 The dimension of a list is always 1! Strictly speaking, the layers do not work with lists, but with arrays. The lists are transferred into a one-dimensional array. Later we will get to know arrays and neural networks with more than one input neuron.

First, we create the first layer, the ***input layer.***

The ***add()*** function and the *layer()* function are used for this.

#Input layer

model.add(layers.Dense(units=3,input_shape=[1]))

The command adds a layer of the type ***Dense to*** the network. *Dense* stands for a dense layer. This means that every neuron within the layer is linked to every neuron of the next layer, and not, for example, to only every second neuron. We also specify the number of neurons (***units***), in our case we choose three neurons.

Input_shape contains, as already mentioned, the dimension of our input list.

Next, we create another layer. We choose two neurons.

#Interlayer

model.add(layers.Dense(units=2))

The layers automatically link to the previous ones. The last layer may only contain one neuron, as this forms the **output layer** and our output list has the dimension one.

#Outputlayer units must be 1

model.add(layers.Dense(units=1))

This is how we built the structure of our network.

The last thing we need to do is ***compile*** our neural network. This is an additional, necessary step. A ***loss function*** must be added to the *compile()* ***function.***

The *loss* function indicates when a deviation should be considered "good" or "bad". As an estimation method we use the assumption that the mean square **error** should be as small as possible.

 This means that a value is called "good" when the deviation from the mean squared becomes minimal. The mean square error is very often used in data processing and is a recognised estimation method in mathematical statistics. It weights outliers from a series of measurements less heavily than other estimation methods.

In addition to the quality criterion for estimating the error, the *compiler* also needs an **optimiser**. We pass an optimisation method to the *optimiser*; by default, we use *SGD (stochastic gradient decent).* The exact mode of operation of an optimiser is unimportant for us. We only need to know that there are different optimisation methods.

```
model.compile(loss='mean_squared_error',optimizer='sgd')
```

The neural network is now *complied* and ready to be trained. To do this, we pass our two data sets to the network with the help of the **fit function**. The input, which forms our list *input,* is called x, the output list *output is called* y.

We also need the number of training runs, which we pass to the variable *epochs.*

```
model.fit(x=input_list,y=output_list,epochs=1000)
```

Now we can run the network for the first time. The console displays the runs at an insane speed. After a few seconds, all 1000 runs should be done. At the end of each line we can see the *loss value.* This is still very large at the beginning and tends towards zero with the number of runs.

```
Console 1/A
Epoch 988/1000
5/5 [==============================] - 0s 196us/step - loss: 0.0714
Epoch 989/1000
5/5 [==============================] - 0s 203us/step - loss: 0.0650
Epoch 990/1000
5/5 [==============================] - 0s 200us/step - loss: 0.0707
Epoch 991/1000
5/5 [==============================] - 0s 196us/step - loss: 0.0643
Epoch 992/1000
5/5 [==============================] - 0s 199us/step - loss: 0.0700
Epoch 993/1000
5/5 [==============================] - 0s 199us/step - loss: 0.0637
Epoch 994/1000
5/5 [==============================] - 0s 0us/step - loss: 0.0692
Epoch 995/1000
5/5 [==============================] - 0s 0us/step - loss: 0.0631
Epoch 996/1000
5/5 [==============================] - 0s 0us/step - loss: 0.0685
Epoch 997/1000
5/5 [==============================] - 0s 196us/step - loss: 0.0624
Epoch 998/1000
5/5 [==============================] - 0s 203us/step - loss: 0.0678
Epoch 999/1000
5/5 [==============================] - 0s 196us/step - loss: 0.0618
Epoch 1000/1000
5/5 [==============================] - 0s 0us/step - loss: 0.0671
```

Figure 62 Console output at 1000 runs

Finally, we want to use our trained net to predict numbers. To do this, we use the **predict()** *command* and pass it one number at a time, in the example we call three *predict()* commands with the numbers 6, 7 and 8.

print(model.predict([6]))

print(model.predict([7]))

print(model.predict([8]))

Before we start the programme, we look at all the code.

from keras import*

model=Sequential()

#Input layer input must be 1

model.add(layers.Dense(units=3,input_shape=[1]))

#Interlayer

model.add(layers.Dense(units=2,input_shape=[1]))

#Outputlayer units must be 1

model.add(layers.Dense(units=1,input_shape=[1]))

```
input_list=[1,2,3,4,5]

output_list=[3,6,9,12,15]

#Creating the network ("adam "alternatively to "sgd")

model.compile(loss='mean_squared_error',optimizer='sgd')

#Training the net 1000 runs

model.fit(x=input_list,y=output_list,epochs=1000)

#Predicting the numbers

print(model.predict([6]))

print(model.predict([7]))

print(model.predict([8]))
```

Then we start the programme. The neural network is trained and after a short time the data to be predicted is output.

```
⊏ Console 1/A
Epoch 998/1000
5/5 [==============================] - 0s 0us/step - loss: 0.0628
Epoch 999/1000
5/5 [==============================] - 0s 0us/step - loss: 0.0574
Epoch 1000/1000
5/5 [==============================] - 0s 203us/step - loss: 0.0622
[[18.452164]]
[[21.533167]]
[[24.614166]]
```

Figure 63 Console output of estimated values

The desired numbers for us were 18, 21 and 24, so we can see that the neural network still has to get much better.

 The neural network becomes more accurate by providing it with more data or by running it more often.

If, for example, we increase the number of runs from 1000 to 10,000, the result becomes much more accurate. The loss value also becomes noticeably smaller.

```
                                                              Help  Varia
⊏ Console 1/A
Epoch 9998/10000
6/6 [==============================] - 0s 0us/step - loss: 6.2735e-07
Epoch 9999/10000
6/6 [==============================] - 0s 0us/step - loss: 6.2771e-07
Epoch 10000/10000
6/6 [==============================] - 0s 0us/step - loss: 6.2735e-07
[[17.998672]]
[[20.998398]]
[[23.998123]]
```

Figure 64 Improvement of estimated values due to higher number of cycles

Depending on the performance of the computer or laptop, 10,000 runs can put a strain on the computer and take a very long time. The programme can be cancelled at any time by pressing the red button in the upper right corner of the console.

It is advisable to play around with the parameters. After how many runs does the result almost no longer improve? Do more layers or more neurons have a positive or negative influence? What happens with other data series?

If the *loss value* or the result shows **"*nan (Not a Number)*"**, there is a numerical error. This can happen relatively quickly with neural networks. There is no uniform solution for this error. In this case, all steps leading to this error should be undone.

Specifying a different optimiser method (*sgd)* can also help. An alternative would be, for example, *optimizer='adam'*

Next, we will process somewhat more complex data. To do this, we first need to understand that the neural network in Python processes arrays and not lists.

7.5. Arrays and numpy

Arrays are a **mathematical construct for** calculating with multi-dimensional variables. In mathematics, these arrays are also called matrices (singular matrix). In Python, the term array, just like lists, is a separate data type. Matrices are very similar to multidimensional lists. However, lists only have one index.

A multi-dimensional list has its own list as an element of this index. An array, on the other hand, has two indices (in the case of a two-dimensional array).

In Spyder we can show the differences very well. To do this, we import the *numpy* library, which contains many numerical functions. Among them are well-known functions such as the exponential function, logarithms or sine and cosine functions. Numpy belongs to the standard libraries that are included in the interpreter. Therefore, we only need to import numpy. Since we only need the *array()* function, only this is imported.

from numpy import array

Next, we look at the concrete difference between multi-dimensional lists and arrays. To do this, we create a data set that shows the salary of a worker depending on age, gender and other factors. With the help of this table and a neural network, we then want to estimate the salary for an arbitrary person.

Age	Duration of education in years	Work experience in years	Gender 0=Man 1= Woman	Monthly salary in €
18	2	0	0	2100
32	4	10	0	3400
44	2	20	0	3200
60	6	34	0	5500
20	2	2	1	2300
24	4	0	1	2700
44	5	21	1	3200
52	2	32	1	3200

 The table only contains random samples. Moreover, important factors such as occupational field are not represented! Nevertheless, the data is perfectly suitable as an example. After all, in reality we can only research samples.

In Python, we first create the data as a two-dimensional list.

```
dataset1=[
    [18,  2,    0,    0,    2100],
    [32,  4,    10,   0,    3400],
    [44,  2,    20,   0,    3200],
    [60,  6,    34,   0,    5500],
    [20,  2,    2,    1,    2300],
    [24,  4,    0,    1,    2700],
    [44,  5,    21,   1,    3200],
    [52,  2,    32,   1,    3200]
]
```

Next, we use the **array()** function **to** form an array from the list.

```
data_array=array(dataset1)
```

In Spyder, we open the Variable Explorer.

| data_array | Array of int32 | (8, 5) | [[18   2   0   0 2100]
[32   4   10   0 3400] |
| dataset1 | list | 8 | [[18, 2, 0, 0, 2100], [32, 4, 10, 0, |

Figure 65 Data type display in Spyder's Variable Explorer

We see the different data types *array* of int32 (integer with 32 bits) and *list*. The difference becomes even clearer if we click on the variable *dataset* as well as on the variable *data_array and* thus open them.

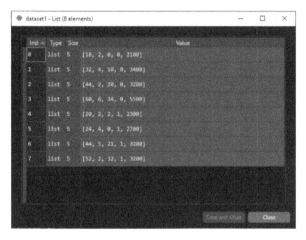

Figure 66 List with 8 elements (one list with 5 elements each)

Figure 67 Array with 8x5 elements

The data of the two data types are identical. An array, on the other hand, has two indices, while a list contains only one index that refers to a complete list.

 It is important for us to understand that neural networks work with arrays and therefore we need to convert our lists into arrays.

Next, we create the data set and create an input variable and an output variable. The input variable contains all the data, the output variable contains the person's salary.

```
input=data_array[0:8,0:4] #All rows (index 0-7) column 0-3
```

```
output=data_array[0:8,4] #All rows column 4
```

We indicate in square brackets our desired rows and our desired columns, each with a comma as separator. With the help of the colons, all elements are used **excluding the** index.

 The dimension of our input vector is four (4 elements per row) and the dimension of the output vector is one (only one element per person, namely the salary).

Accordingly, we create our neural network.

This time we create a total of four layers: one input layer, one output layer and two intermediate layers. Also, this time we assign significantly more neurons per layer: 16 for the input layer, 64 for the intermediate layers and one for the output layer.

```
model=Sequential()
```

```
#Input layer input must be 4
```

```
model.add(layers.Dense(units=16,input_shape=[4]))
```

```
#Interlayer
```

```
model.add(layers.Dense(units=64))
```

```
model.add(layers.Dense(units=64))
```

```
#Outputlayer units must be 1
```

```
model.add(layers.Dense(units=1))
```

Next, we *compile* the network and then train it. This time the optimiser *adam* is used. In addition, the cycles have been increased to 5000. Depending on the computing power, the training can take a few minutes.

```
#Compiling the network
```

```
model.compile(loss='mean_squared_error',optimizer='adam')
```

```
#Training the network with 5000 runs
```

```
model.fit(x=input,y=output,epochs=5000)
```

The last part is the exciting part. We want to estimate the salary of a person who does not appear in the data set.

To do this, we create two test persons, *pers1* and *pers2*.

Tom is male, 18 years old, has a one-year apprenticeship and correspondingly one year of work experience.

Lisa is female, 52 years old, has seven years of education and already 20 years of work experience.

```
#Predicting the numbers
tom=array([[18,1,1,0]])
lisa=array([[52,7,20,1]])
print(model.predict(tom))
print(model.predict(lisa))
```

When we start the programme, the network is trained. As a result, we get afterwards:

```
Epoch 4999/5000
8/8 [==============================] - 0s 249us/step - loss: 81841.4609
Epoch 5000/5000
8/8 [==============================] - 0s 125us/step - loss: 81839.5859
[[1920.1534]]
[[4837.581]]
```

Figure 68 Estimated salary of Tom and Lisa

The estimated monthly salary for Tim is 1920€ and for Lisa 4838 €.

-·Ọ́·-   Our neural network evaluated the four factors and estimated a potential salary based on this data.

The AI can also evaluate the individual influences of the input data.

Does the data set show unequal pay based on gender? To test this thesis, we again create two individuals, Niklas and Jennifer. Both are 30 years old, have three years of education and seven years of work experience. The only difference we set in the data is gender.

```
niklas=array([[30,3,7,0]])
jennifer=array([[30,3,7,1]])
print(model.predict(niklas))
print(model.predict(jennifer))
```

Again, we run the neural network and get a monthly salary for Niklas of €3059 and for Jennifer of €2570.

```
Epoch 5000/5000
8/8 [==============================] - 0s 127us/step - loss: 79294.7188
[[3058.8115]]
[[2569.4277]]
```

Figure 69 Dependence of gender on estimated salary

The correlation that gender affects salary can be reproduced without doubt. This could not be clearly proven on the basis of the measurement data.

 Other influencing variables such as different age, work experience etc. can also be tested.

We must always keep in mind that all estimates are made on the basis of samples only. Perhaps we had randomly selected non-representative samples.

 To be able to make a reliable statement, we need significantly more data.

"Data is the new oil"

EU politician Meglena Kuneva - 2009

This concludes our insight into the world of neural networks. We have learned how a neural network is constructed and how to program a simple neural network in Python. We have also seen that the accuracy depends considerably on the computational effort and the data fed into it.

In summary, we have worked through all the essential parts of Python programming. We worked through the basics, learned about classes and objects and even touched on artificial intelligence.

Of course, the Python universe is even more extensive and there are countless modules, interfaces to other programmes and much more. In any case, after reading this book, more than the foundation should now be laid. In this sense: Happy programming!

Free eBook

Thank you for buying this book. Since the printing of the book is done directly by Amazon and I have no influence on the quality of the images, it is possible that some details may be lost.

That's why I offer the eBook for free as a PDF file when you buy the book. There, all the pictures are in high resolution and you always get the latest version.

To do so, send a message with the subject "Python3 EN", as well as a screenshot of the purchase or proof of the order at Amazon to the email:

Benjamin-Spahic@web.de

I will send you the eBook and the programme codes immediately.

If you are missing something, don't like it or have suggestions for improvement or questions, feel free to send me an email.

Constructive criticism is important in order to be able to improve something. I am constantly revising the book and am happy to respond to any constructive suggestions for improvement.

Otherwise, if you liked the book, I would also appreciate a positive review on Amazon. That helps the visibility of the book and is the greatest praise an author can receive.

Your Benjamin

About the author

Benjamin Spahic was born in Heidelberg in 1995 and grew up in a village with 8,000 inhabitants near Karlsruhe. His passion for technology is reflected in his studies as an electrical engineer with a focus on information technology at the University of Applied Sciences in Karlsruhe.

He then deepened his knowledge in the field of regenerative energy production at the Karlsruhe University of Applied Sciences.

Disclaimer

The author assumes no responsibility for the topicality, completeness and correctness of the information provided. Furthermore, no guarantee can be given for the achievement of the described skills.

Photo credits:

Icons:
https://icons8.de/icon/113140/kugelbirne
https://icons8.de/icon/79638/obligatorische
https://icons8.de/icon/78038/math
https://icons8.de/icon/42314/taschenrechner

All non-mentioned contents were created by the author himself. He is therefore the author of the graphics and has the rights of use and distribution.

*: *https://docs.python.org/3/library/functions.html*
*: *https://www.python.org/community/logos/*
**: *https://en.wikipedia.org/wiki/File:Datove_centrum_TCP.jpg*
**: *https://pixabay.com/de/vectors/schaltungen-gehirn-netzwerk-chip-5076888/*

* *This file is made available under the GNU Free Documentation License.*

https://commons.wikimedia.org/wiki/Commons:GNU_Free_Documentation_License,_version_1.2Es may have been modified.
** *This file is made available under the Creative Commons licence "CC0 1.0 waiver of copyright".*

https://creativecommons.org/publicdomain/zero/1.0/deed.deEs changes may have been made.

www.ingramcontent.com/pod-product-compliance
Lightning Source LLC
LaVergne TN
LVHW051654050326
832903LV00032B/3799